The MYSTERY FANcier

Volume 9, Number 2
March/April 1987

The Mystery Fancier

Volume 9, Number 2
March/April 1987

TABLE OF CONTENTS

MYSTERIOUSLY SPEAKING   Page 1

In Memorium: John Nieminski   Page 3
    By Ely Liebow

Mystery Mosts   Pages 6, 7, 8
    By Jeff Banks

A Consummation Devoutly to Be Wished   ·Page 9
    Joe R. Christopher

The Cream of Queen   Page 20
    By Frank Floyd

Further Gems from the Literature   Page 21
    By William F. Deeck

IT'S ABOUT CRIME   Page 24
    By Marvin Lachman

REEL MURDERS   Page 31
    By Walter Albert

VERDICTS   Page 33
    Book Reviews

THE DOCUMENTS IN THE CASE   Page 45
    Letters

The Mystery Fancier
(USPS: 428-590)
is edited and published by-monthly by
Guy M. Townsend
1711 Clifty Drive
Madison, IN   47250

SUBSCRIPTION RATES: Second-class mail, U.S. and Canada,
$15.00 per year (6 issues); first-class mail, U.S. and Canada,
$18.00; overseas surface mail, $15.00; overseas air mail, $21.00.
Overseas subscribers please pay in international money order,
check drawn on U.S. bank, or currency; no checks drawn on
foreign banks, please.

WILDSIDE PRESS

Mysteriously Speaking ...

For a change, I'm typing these comments after all of the rest of the issue is in the computer, and I have only left myself this page and the next for my remarks. For another change, this issue is so appallingly late that I figured a few more days wouldn't matter, so I have taken a few hours to read through the copy and do a bit of editing (the editing is the change, of course; not the lateness). As a result, there should be noticeably fewer typos and blank lines, though I have tried to keep my editing of the actual copy to an absolute minimum. Though otherwise a good thing, this confining myself to two pages has its down side, because there are a number of things that I would like to mention which I will have to slight or skip altogether. And if I keep on explaining like this I'll use up all my space without getting anything said at all. So here goes.

BOWLING GREEN UNIVERSITY POPULAR PRESS

Bowling Green's Pat and Ray Browne continue to hold their own as the most prolific publishers of secondary works in the mystery field. In the introduction to his own collection of fifteen essays, *Heroes and Humanities: Detective Fiction and Culture* (1987, 141 pp., $8.95/$19.95), Ray Browne writes that "in this book I have deliberately avoided those giants of American suspense fiction--such as Hammett and Chandler, the two Mac-donalds, Rex Stout, Robert Parker, and scores of others. Instead I have been concerned with a rather carefully chosen group whose works so far, for one reason or another, have been pretty well overlooked and neglected." Putting aside my own astonishment at discovering that anyone in this universe, except Parker himself, of course, would put Robert B. Parker in the same class as Hammett, Chandler, Stout, and John D. and Ross, I'm bound to say that this is an interesting collection and well worth the paperback price (the eleven extra dollars for the hard cover edition causes my heart to race). Also just out from Bowling Green is a book whose title virtually guarantees that I'll never read it--*In Search of the Paper Tiger: A Sociological Perspective of Myth, Formula, and the Mystery Genre in the Entertainment Print Mass Medium.* The book, whose author is Gary Hoppenstand and whose price is $8.95/$19.95 (and, while I'm being awkward, whose page count is 134 and whose publication date was 1 April

1987), may be the greatest work in the mystery field since *A Catalogue of Crime*, but I stopped reading books with dissertation-style titles a long time back, and it's a bad habit I'm glad to be rid of. The third recent Popular Press release--B.A. Pike's *Campion's Career: A Study of the Novels of Margery Allingham* (1987, 253 pp., $13.95/$26.95)--is another story. This is the kind of scholarship that made the early TAD sparkle, before a surfeit of pretentious Ph.D.s started using its pages to try to justify their interest in mysteries (which, as any right thinking human knows, needs no justification at all) by reading cosmic significance into the genre. Give me the honest, enthusiastic scholarship of, say, Bob Sampson, to the precious claptrap of one of the P(iled) h(igher and) D(eeper) boys any day. (As a matter of fact, Barry Pike may be a professor of English and may even hold a Ph.D., but he doesn't wear it on his sleeve, which is the point of this diatribe; it is, after all, possible to be educated without being insufferable--damned difficult, maybe, but still possible.)

MYSTERIOUS PRESS

Since envy is a sin, Otto Penzler must bear at least some responsibility for the direction in which my soul is headed. Every time I turn around I stumble over yet another successful Penzler enterprize. The most recent revolting development is Otto's "Mysterious Library," a wonderful line of trade paperbacks which includes Bill Pronzini's *Gun in Cheek* ($8.95), *Raymond Chandler's Unknown Thriller: The Screenplay of Playback* [with an introduction by God himself: "One could speculate that Chandler's enthusiasm for the Dulwich education is possible only if it ignores the degree to which the sexual sublimation it required may have exacerbated the atypical situation of his home life. And one probably should so speculate. But not here."] ($9.95), *Ross Macdonald's Inward Journey: Reflections on Ross Macdonald by 25 of America's Most Distinguished Authors* [including, of course, God himself: "I never met him personally."], edited by Ralph B. Sipper ($8.95), and *The Eyes Have It: The First Private Eye Writers of America Anthology*, edited by Robert J. Randisi ($8.95). I'm consoling myself with the thought that I am taller than Otto--though not, perhaps, as tall as God himself.

CLIFFHANGER PRESS

I am pleased to report that the U.S. Postal Service was just joshing me when it returned my letter to Cliffhanger Press as "not deliverable as addressed--unable to forward." What a sense of humor those boys have. I read Frank Free's *Fly from Evil* (1986, $6.95 [quality trade paperback]) with rapt attention. Its main character is as irritating a mixture of good and bad as I've come across in a long while, and Free's ideas on international travel bear no relation whatever to the real world, but I'm looking forward to the promised sequel. I've not yet gotten around to *A Killing in Real Estate*, by Rudd Brown (also 1986 and $6.95).

In Memorium: John Nieminski

Ely Liebow

John Nieminski was the third delectable mountain (to paraphrase John Bunyan) in my life to die suddenly, leaving me
gasping for breath and looking for answers. The first two, an
old Navy buddy and a phys. ed. teacher at Northeastern, were
both ebullient, witty, larger-than-life types. John was witty
enough, but one of those quiet dependable solid people whose
wit, charm, and humanity sneak up on you.
  I remember well sitting down on my daughter's bed in her
darkened bedroom after talking to John's son and his wife,
Joyce, the night of December 19. In the dark, the room began
spinning and everything seemed to be beyond understanding. I
had just talked to John in the morning, telling him about our
new hotel, the Dumont Plaza, in New York for the BSI weekend.
As usual, he joked about it. "Make sure it's a *confirmed*
reservation," he said, remembering our hassle at the San
Francisco Bouchercon a couple of years ago. I could think only
of the dirges spoken or sung over the great and lovely souls of
the past. John was my friend, faithful and just to me.

"But O the heavy change now thou art gone,
"Now thou art gone and never must return."

  I guess that's it. John's passing brought about a heavy
change in many lives, for among all the aficionados, cogni-
scienti, lovers of detective fiction, science fiction, old-time-
radio, the sports pages, and, by Zeus, even classical traditional
literature, John was right up there on the top. He loved the
printed word and had absolutely immersed himself in the classic
and modern mystery, the early and contemporary science fiction,
Dickens, Shaw, Boswell and Johnson, and even Virginia Woolf.
  When I became a member of Hugo's Companions nearly two
decades ago, John was The Most Drunken Companion--or
secretary. I was fortunate, indeed, for I wrote him, asking
about the rules and regulations of that august body. His reply
was typical of all of John's writing: graceful, honest, and to the
point. I was so taken by the spirit, grace, and panache of the
letter that I asked if we couldn't meet a half-hour or so earlier
than the next meeting. He agreed, and we began meeting
irregularly thereafter. He became my friend John Nieminski,

rather that "just" a Sherlockian, and I think that is true with
nearly everyone who really got to know John. For a man who
was relatively quiet, soft spoken, and modest on the outside, he
became a witty, warm, comfortable friend. Like most men, John
didn't bare his soul or expound on his personal life, yet like so
many of John's DAPA-EM, Sherlockian, and Bouchercon friends,
I feel I knew John better than I know most men, because we
caught him in the midst of all his loves and enthusiasms. Like
Richard Cory, John had a glitter in his walk and talk when
engaged in any literary discussion, and I guess that's how many
remember him best.

In fact, it was John who first mentioned a "non-academic"
convention to me. In the early seventies he asked me how I'd
like to go to the Popular Culture Convention in Milwaukee.
When I asked him what it was, he said one couldn't describe or
define it, one had to see it in the flesh. He did mention that it
might hold some pleasant surprises for me. Sure enough, one of
the first things I saw at the newly refurbished Shroeder Hotel
was a display of books by various publishers. There were all
kinds of books--texts and otherwise--on detective fiction. I
remember how eager he was to take me to the display, and how
he observed my every reaction.

"Well," he grinned, "what do you think?"

"John, do people really teach detective fiction?"

"It might be the world's second oldest profession," he said.

I was enthralled. I began talking to all the book dealers.
"John," I asked, knowing exactly what the answer would be, "do
you know anyone who teaches detective fiction?"

"There are several people, but why don't you write to
Randy Cox at St. Olaf's. He's a librarian who's been teaching
it, and I'm sure he can give you some advice."

I don't believe I ever came to John with a question dealing
with detective fiction that he didn't or couldn't answer. In
fact, at the same P-C convention, John and I sat in on an
Ellery Queen panel. It was very informal and the three Queen
experts sat us all in a big circle. Several times the experts
were stumped by a date or publication, and confused by a
question. Each time they called on John and he came up with
the answer. It was such an awesome performance, I nearly
began to think everything was fixed. A year or so later John's
superb bibliography to EQMM was published. In talking about it
with me, he told me he had never subscribed to the magazine.
He always bought it at the newsstand or book store. In fact,
John probably spent more time in book stores on his lunch hour
than anyone in North America. A few years later at a BSI
weekend, he told me, with unusual excitement in his voice, that
Don Yates was taking him somewhere really special for lunch.
Don took him to the editorial offices of EQMM where he met
Eleanor Sullivan, among others. It was as though the White Sox
had just won the pennant and the Bears beat the Redskins again
73-0. That's all he talked about on the plane ride back to
Chicago.

I have no idea when I first met John's DAPA-EM friends.
It had to have been at an early Bouchercon. They filled the

skies like the locusts in "The Good Earth." They came up out
of the ground, covering everything. They were—to the un-
initiated—an enthusiastic, amazingly knowledgeable bunch of
detective fiction nuts who regaled one another with bi-monthly
newsletters, daily letters, and hourly phone calls. There has
probably not been such an intrepid, enthusiastic bunch since
Lenin invited a few of the boys over to his basement in 1916.
John's newsletter—or apazine—was aptly entitled *Somewhere a
Roscoe*, a term straight out of S.J. Perelman. Having grown up,
been weaned, and teethed on people like Perelman and H.L.
Mencken, I was not surprised in the least that John too reveled
in them. I will be eternally grateful to the patron saint of
serendipity, St. Stanislaus, that John, Art Scott, and I decided
to visit Mencken's home—now a city monument—in Baltimore at
last year's Bouchercon. It was a quiet, thoroughly satisfying
experience.

From John, his mother, and his family I learned that he
was an inveterate reader at the age of four when he went out
to Comiskey Park and was determined to learn the names (in
print) of his White Sox heroes. John's father ran a Polish radio
station back in the thirties, and John, we are told, knew Polish
perfectly when he was three. At the age of five he apparently
learned to read box scores and started losing his Polish.

John and I had many of the same horsehide heroes: Jimmy
Foxx, Zeke Bonura, Nellie Fox, Ted Williams, and Luke Appling.
We both hated the Yankees with a passion. He found it hard to
believe that I was in my $9 season-ticket seat at Griffith
Stadium in 1940 when his burly Bears defeated my beloved
Redskins 73-0 for the old NFL championship. He was always
looking for the scars.

In addition to baseball, John loved games and was instru-
mental in fostering, starting, aiding, and abetting such games as
gossamer, Sherlockian song titles, etc. Many years ago the two
of us were on a nearly empty plane to Culver City, California,
and were discussing all the information provided on the back of
baseball cards, especially the weird-sounding home towns of the
ball players. A few years later, on another plane, he looked
over at me and said out of nowhere, "Paw Paw, Michigan."

I blinked, grinned, and shot back, "Charley Maxwell," and
we were off.

There were two things—well, perhaps one—that not too
many of his friends knew about John. On two strange ("outre"
would be a better word) occasions, the members of the all-male
Hugo's Companions voted on 1) whether to allow a female to
attend one of its irregular meetings, and 2) whether to admit a
superbly gifted female as a member. On both occasions quiet,
pleasant, scholarly John Nieminski became their champion. He
was soft-spoken, logical, eloquent. I'll never forget how
surprised and impressed I was. He did the same once when
recommending a long-standing, faithful Companion for the
position of Sir Hugo. He had nothing against the eventual
winner, but he felt that common sense, loyalty, and the choice
of candidates dictated his choice. Again, he presented a most
subdued, eloquent argument.

The other trait or characteristic was John's attention to
detail, his sense of duty. I could not get over how impressed a
printer was when John showed him his concept for the cover of
the Bouchercon XV program. He couldn't believe John hadn't
used fancy equipment. On many an occasion he would ask my
opinion of a hot-off-the-press *Baker Street Miscellanea*.
Knowing how he took such pains for perfection, I would give
the new magazine a close study. Inevitably I found nothing
wrong. "But they didn't cut the tops evenly," or "That cover's
a shade darker than the last one," he would say. There was no
better editor for anything than John Nieminski.

I thought I'd miss John terribly at the BSI weekend this
year, but (a) we went to a strange, half-finished, new hotel; (b)
four of us were sharing fairly cramped quarters and we flipped
for the two regular, comfortable beds (in retrospect I think we
also flipped cramped quarters); I shared my pull-out couch the
first night with a female, the second night with a male from
California (I am nothing if not multi-faceted); George Armstrong
slept on a roll-away cot; nails, which we could not hammer in
with bricks, protruded from the carpeting. We were definitely
cramped, but if John Nieminski had been with us, believe me, it
would have been a much bigger place.

MYSTERY MOSTS: MAGAZINES

The longest-running magazine specializing in mystery
fiction is--you guessed it!--*Ellery Queen's Mystery Magazine*.
EQMM will finish forty-six years of publication with its
September 1987 issue, which should appear soon after this does.
Just like Walter Payton in the NFL, who extends his record
every time he handles the ball, the magazine has been adding to
its age record with each month of continuing publication for
about three years now.

The runner-up, *Street & Smith's Detective Story Magazine*,
was the first "specialized" pulp magazine, and the first magazine
other than various dime novel "libraries" and "weeklies" to
specialize in mystery fiction. DSM lasted just three or four
months shy of thirty-four years.

Among the dime novel story papers *Old Sleuth Library* was
the longest running, with a mystery specialization under a single
title, and the first to specialize in "our" field. It lasted twenty
years, mostly on a quarterly schedule. *Nick Carter's*, published
consecutively (though under a succession of three different
titles), lasted just over twenty-four years.

The runner-up among contemporary mystery magazines (and
third overall) is EQMM's companion, *Alfred Hitchcock's Mystery
Magazine*. At thirty years old, AHMM will supplant DSM in
overall second place in the early 1990s.

Only three magazines have attained the ripe old age of
thirty. (Jeff Banks)

Mystery Mosts: Most Performances

Jeff Banks

One immediately thinks of Raymond Burr's almost two hundred portrayals of Perry Mason when considering actors' identification with detective roles. But this was far from the most frequent portrayal of any detective hero by a single actor. William Gillette, one of the first successful and by far the most enduring stage Holmes, performed the play he adapted from several Doyle short stories more than thirteen hundred times on stage, once as a silent film, and several times on radio. Surely nothing could top that, you say, even though this was a single *performance* repeated ad infinitum.

You are wrong.

Basil Rathbone appeared as Holmes in fourteen *different* films, plus a cameo appearance in the 1943 comedy *Crazy House*, in three performances of a stage play written by his wife, and in some 270 radio episodes for the longest (seven year) run of any radio Holmes. The Rathbone total, approaching three hundred portrayals, is still far short of Gillette's mark. His partner, Nigel Bruce, did all those shows (except the stage show) as his Watson, plus an additional radio season, likely making him the champion Watson, with over three hundred performances.

However, thinking radio puts you on the right trace. Brett Morrison, the longest-running Lamont Cranston, adding occasional cameo appearances to a nine-year regular tenure, passed the 350 mark as The Shadow. Jay Jostyn played *Mr. District Attorney* about 550 times in an eleven-year radio run; the show took no summer vacations and was rarely pre-empted. He also did that role first on TV. *Mr. District Attorney* began as a nightly serial starring another actor, and it saw about seven hundred episodes in each format. *Mr. Keen, Tracer of Lost Persons* had a similar (and even longer!) history--a three-times-a-week serial for its first six years, and a nightly run for its last three. It saw at least fifteen hundred episodes in the various formats, including at least eight years of once-a-week shows. Bennett Kilpatrick played "the kindly old tracer" longer and more times (about one thousand) than any other actor; even he did not top Gillette's Holmes.

Ambiguities in information available on daily serial casts make it impossible to say definitely which of these super radio stars actually had the most episodes as heroes in their longest-run roles. John Larkin, the last Perry Mason; Bennett Kilpatrick, the original Mr. Keen (Tracer of Lost Persons); Staats Cotsworth, the longest-running "Front Page" Farrell--each of these had fifteen hundred to two thousand appearances, eclipsing even Gillette's Holmes. Larkin was also a supporting player on *Under Arrest* and the title character for a time of *Mark Trail* (a borderline juvenile series). His other genre work included being the last radio Buck Rogers, and of course his being a major featured player for more than half a decade on half a dozen of the most popular women's serials (soap operas) gave him at least a tenuous connection with mystery for it was ever a prominent plot ingredient. He finished out his acting career as the original Adam Drake of TV's *Edge of Night*, the soap in the visual medium most steeped in mystery. With a minimum of sixteen hundred Mason appearances, he is the most likely champion of them all.

Kilpatrick otherwise acted exclusively on radio soaps, for the most part with smaller roles but over about twice the time span of Larkin's career. But Cotsworth, even if behind the other two (as he may *not* have been) in appearances in a single role, surely played more episodes as heroes than any other actor. Though he also had soap roles, was featured support on some mystery shows, and followed Larkin as Mark Trail, he is best known for his twelve year run as Casey, Crime Photographer, in the show of the same name. He made upwards of six hundred weekly appearances as Casey and more than two hundred daily ones (in its final year). So just the two newsman-detective hero roles gave Cotsworth at least twenty-three hundred appearances, and he may have even reached three thousand.

[Ironically, one of the first articles I need to use a "Mystery Most" on is Jeff's own "Mystery Most" intro.]

Mystery Mosts: Long Careers

About twenty mystery writers kept delighting us for more than thirty-five years. Among them, Sax Rohmer, Anna Katherine Green, and John Creasey all exceeded forty-five. But the real champions passed the half-century mark.

These were Agatha Christie and Leslie Charteris, who both reached fifty-two years if we include Christie's posthumous publications. Lester Dent, most of whose Doc Savage books published under the house name Kenneth Robeson appeared posthumously, bettered that by a year. And Walter B. Gibson, most of whose Shadow novels appeared under the house name Maxwell Grant, reached fifty-four years in 1985. There is a good chance that more Dent/Robeson and Gibson/Grant books will appear posthumously in the future. Of course, Charteris's career spanned longer than that of any other writer during his lifetime. (Jeff Banks)

A Consummation Devoutly to Be Wished: Four More Collections of Anthony Boucher's Mysteries

Joe R. Christopher

One of the happiest things which happened to me in 1983 was the discovery that a collection of Anthony Boucher's mystery stories, including all of the Nick Noble tales, was appearing. I walked around for three days in sheer delight.

And I got *Exeunt Murderers* and continued to be pleased with it, even if the first excitement wore off. Let me restrict myself to this book's presentation of the Nick Noble stories and show that I can be, to a degree, objective. Someone—one of the editors, presumably, and I would guess Mike Nevins (Francis M. Nevins, Jr., on the title page)—called this part of the book "An Ennead of Nobles." That is delightful, and it suggests Boucher's fondness for recondite diction.

But let me imagine that sometime in the future, after *Exeunt Murderers* is O.P., a publisher decides on (say) a trade paperback of the stories about Nick Noble. I think "An Ennead of Nobles" is much more a division title than a book title. I hope that the future publisher will go to Ellery Queen's suggestion in *In the Queen's Parlor*, Leaf 17: "Any of the classic short story titles would fit:
> The Adventures of Nick Noble
> The Case Book of Nick Noble
Or perhaps the publishers would prefer a more orthodox title—
> Noble Experiments
> Noble Obliges."
My vote goes for that last, perfect title. Besides the pun, it catches the fact that the policemen go to Noble with their cases and he obliges by seeing the hidden pattern—and thus the solution.

I've got a quibble about the biographical listing of Nick Noble, "From *Detective's Who's Who*," which follows "Screwball Division" (the first story). I haven't seen that story's first publication, in *Ellery Queen's Mystery Magazine* in 1942, but I believe that listing was invented for the reprinting of the story in Boucher's anthology *Four and Twenty Bloodhounds* (1950), since Boucher requested like listings from the other authors. My guess is that the editors photocopied the story in the anthology and picked up the biographical listing. If that is so (the book, however, gives no 1950 copyright for the brief item), then the placement is purely arbitrary. It could have, here, been placed on page two, opposite the start of the first story. In that future volume it might be placed on a separate recto page at the front of the volume, giving Noble's biography before the stories start.

By the way, this bibliographical sketch refers to this first story as "The 7:06 Murders." I've sometimes wondered if Boucher might not have intended to retitle the story this way and call his eventual collection *Screwball Division* or maybe, in a phrase from the story, *Screwball Division, L.A.P.D.* That would be a good title, too. (The same, fuller version of this phrase reappears in the last story, "The Girl Who Married a Monster.")

The mention of *Four and Twenty Bloodhounds* reminds me that in it Boucher has a brief introduction to "Screwball Division", giving the sources of some of the story's details. In another M.W.A. anthology, *Eat, Drink, and Be Buried* (1956), edited by Rex Stout, Boucher has an afterword to another Noble story, "Crime Must Have a Stop," discussing the story's weaknesses and strengths. And in yet another, *Butcher, Baker, Murder-Maker* (1954), edited by George Harmon Coxe, Boucher introduces "The Girl Who Married a Monster" with a comment on the source of the plot. (I haven't seen one of the Noble stories in another anthology to learn if Boucher has another such comment in it--*Planned Departures* [1958], edited by Michael Gilbert, is a [British] Crime Writers' Association book, with "Like Count Palmieri" in it.) *Exeunt Murderers* preserves two introductions to non-series stories, and if such an introduction or afterword is headed by such a term with the date of its publication--"Introduction (1950)"--and if the comments are set in italics to contrast them with the story, then I think they are acceptable in a collection. (It's a pity, however, that the *first* story in a Noble collection has an introduction, since that tosses comments about the stories, rather than the fiction itself, at the reader at the beginning.) A few readers will be turned off by these introductions and afterwords, but the more serious fans will love them--and probably most readers won't care one way or another. And, after all, it is that combination of general readers and serious fans which give certain works in a field their staying power.

But despite the fact that *Exeunt Murderers* does not (to my mind) properly place the biographical sketch and does not preserve Boucher's comments on his stories, those are small matters compared to the fact that the editors rescue "The Punt and the Pass" from its obscurity in a 1945 issue of *Short Stories* and "Death of a Patriarch" from Ellery Queen's filing cabinet--it was purchased by E.Q.M.M. but never published. (The "Author's Note" which Boucher wrote to follow "Death of a Patriarch" should, as here, do precisely that in that imagined separate edition.)

Looking at Nevins' checklist of Boucher's fiction in the back of the book, I see that two of the Noble stories, in addition to the four I've mentioned, have been reprinted in one or more anthologies. Most fans would be aware of some of

them at least, even if the fans' reading doesn't go back to the
original E.Q.M.M. appearances in the forties and early fifties.
That leaves "The Punt, and the Pass," "Death of a Patriarch" (of
course), and "Rumor, Inc." as the unreprinted stories. The
latter was probably not picked up because of its partial nature
as a World War II propaganda piece. But "The Punt and the
Pass" is one of the best stories, and it is very good to have it
generally available at last.

More could be said about the Noble tales, but that would
probably lead me into detailed consideration of literary aspects,
and I want to write about book collections in this note, not
even about the detectives *per se*. (I have given almost no
details about Noble himself in the foregoing comments.) What I
want to propose are four more collections, to supplement *Exeunt
Murderers'* "An Ennead of Nobles." I should make it clear that
I am not just proposing that the rest of Boucher's mystery
stories be collected. There are eight or nine of those (perhaps
a few more if one includes some of Boucher's SF and fantasy
stories with mystery elements), and they may be chased down
through Nevins' bibliography. I would be delighted if they were
collected, but that would be one volume, not four.

LAMB, WITH MINT SAUCE

Boucher's first mystery novel, *The Case of the Seven of
Calvary* (1937), involved Martin Lamb, whom Mike Nevins calls
"a transparent stand-in for Boucher himself" (*Exeunt Murderers*,
p. ix). The novel is set on the campus of the University of
California at Berkeley, with Lamb playing Watson to the
Holmesian Sanskrit scholar, Dr. John Ashwin. This is probably
the only mystery novel in existence which begins its first
chapter with a line of Sanskrit. (By the way, I *do* realize that
"Dr. John Ashwin" sounds more like Dr. John Watson, syllable
for syllable, than it does like Sherlock Holmes.)

Boucher never followed up that novel with another about
Lamb (or about Ashwin, for that matter), but he wrote several
short stories in which Lamb figures:
"The Way I Heard It" (1944)
"Toy Cassowary" (1945)
"The Anomaly of the Empty Man" (1952, revised 1953)
"Nellthu" (1955)
The first two and the fourth are short shorts and are super-
natural stories involving a ghost, a voodoo priest, and a demon,
respectively. Nevins does not mark the fourth story as involving Lamb in his bibliography, but the protagonist is called
Martin and he meets a woman, Ailsa, whom he had known at
"the University" almost twenty-five years before--and 25 from
1955 is 1930. Admittedly, *The Case of the Seven of Calvary*
appeared in 1937, but if a critic stresses the "almost" in the
twenty-five years, if he or she notes that in the novel Lamb is
a research fellow in German (presumably something like a
graduate assistant), and if he or she assumes that Martin and
Ailsa met when they were undergraduates, then the chronology

is manageable. So I assume "Nellthu" belongs with the rest. Certainly Lamb's amorousness in "Nellthu" matches his in *The Case of the Seven of Calvary.* (I do not assume that Lamb has to be Boucher's "stand-in" in all details of the fiction.)

Since there are only one novel and four stories, what I'd like to suggest is a collection containing them all. Omnibuses often contain three novels these days (and up to five), and trade paperbacks have sometimes gathered two or three novels, so the proposal is not too startling.

I have played with titles for this book. Years ago, when Bob Briney, the late Dean Dickensheet, and I did an annotated Boucher bibliography for the early *Armchair Detective,* I called the section on Lamb "Alias Watson: The Memoirs of Martin Lamb." Lamb clearly plays the role of Watson in the novel and the third short story, and he is something of an onlooker in the other stories; but for a book title "Alias Watson" would probably be misleading. I have thought about a couple of others--

The Observations of Martin Lamb
The Mysterious Career of Martin Lamb.

But, of course, what I would prefer is the title I used for this section--

Lamb, with Mint Sauce.

I don't really expect that a publisher would agree to the latter, although it suggests Boucher's delight in good food, for it would not "call" the right audience. But it seems to me (and perhaps only to me) delightfully clever.

I have two bibliographic suggestions for this book. First, in our old bibliography, Dickensheet pointed out that Boucher changed the dedication to *The Case of the Seven of Calvary* after his model for Dr. Ashwin died, to name the person directly. I think the collection should contain both dedications, labeled "Dedication to the first edition," and "Dedication to the third edition." (Perhaps I should explain that I did only the long first draft of the bibliography and wasn't involved in the rest, so I didn't know who contributed what to it; but Briney replied to a first draft of this essay with a letter--1 July 1986-- saying that Dickensheet was responsible here and in another passage below.)

Second, "The Anomaly of the Empty Man" has an interesting preface, mainly about Boucher's attitudes toward San Francisco, found with its second (revised) appearance, in *Crook's Tour* (1953), an M.W.A. anthology edited by Bruno Fischer. This three-paragraph note was obviously inspired by the geographic thesis of Fischer's anthology, but it is worth reprinting--both for this imagined volume and, even more thematically, in the last volume which is suggested in this essay.

Would this volume have some appeal beyond that to Boucher fans and historically minded mystery fans? I think so. Obviously, Boucher's fair-play puzzle and his fantasies would appeal to two different audiences; but I have avoided discussing the content of "The Anomaly of the Empty Man" so far. As surely most readers of this magazine know, it is one of those detective tales with two solutions, one natural, one super-natural--the kind of story Frank D. McSherry, Jr., discusses in

his essay "The Janus Resolution" (1968, rev. 1970). But even
more important, in it Lamb visits Dr. Horace Verner, Sherlock
Holmes' cousin as mentioned in the Canon; and one episode is a
flashback with Verner and Holmes in London in the year of
Queen Victoria's death. This is certainly Boucher's greatest
Sherlockian fiction and, I believe, one of the best of all the
short story pastiches. A publisher playing this up in his ads
should be able to increase his sales substantially to Holmesian
collectors, even though the story has previously been printed in
Boucher's first science fiction and fantasy collection, *Far and
Away* (1955).

THE CASEBOOK OF FERGUS O'BREEN

With his second novel, Boucher introduced a Los Angeles
private eye, Fergus O'Breen. The novels in which he appears
are:

The Case of the Crumpled Knave (1939)
The Case of the Solid Key (1941)
The Case of the Seven Sneezes (1942)

Boucher followed these up with the following novelettes, short
stories, and short short:

"The Compleat Werewolf" (1942)
"Elsewhen" (1943)
"The Last Hand" (written 1945, published 1958)
"The Chronokinesis of Jonathan Hull" (1946)
"The Pink Caterpillar" (1951)
"Gandolphus" (1952, revised 1956)
"The Ultimate Clue" (1960)

There is also another O'Breen story, which Nevins calls a
novelette version of *The Case of the Crumpled Knave*:

"The Clue of the Knave of Diamonds" (published 1963)

Actually, as Dickensheet pointed out in our bibliography, this is
the original version of the novel—and it is really novel length.
(It was crammed into one issue of E.Q.M.M. with very small
print.) As I remember, one of the main differences is that Col.
Theodore Rand is not treated humorously in this original
version; he was rewritten for the novel in what sounds to me
like an imitation of Carter Dickson's H.M.

Obviously, what I am suggesting is a collection of the
Fergus O'Breen stories. I called it *The Casebook of* in my
section title because the novels are all called *The Case of the
Adjective Noun*, and I thought the partial echo of *Case* in
Casebook was appropriate.

I have no authorial additions to this book in the form of
forewords or afterwords. Ellery Queen (Frederic Dannay) has an
afterword to the E.Q.M.M. publication of "The Last Hand,"
discussing the gimmick Boucher used in the story—defending it,
actually. I do not know if that editorial afterword was reprinted with the story in the one anthology appearance which
Nevins lists, but the story does turn on a curious technicality.

Of the shorter O'Breen fiction, "The Compleat Werewolf"
and "The Pink Caterpillar" are fantasies; "Elsewhen," "The

Chronokinesis of Jonathan Hull," and "Gandolphus" are science fiction; and "The Last Hand" (as suggested above) and "The Ultimate Clue" are mysteries. (It's odd how the fantasies and the mysteries have titles of "The Adjective Noun" pattern, tempting one to add "The Case of" in front of them, but none of the science fiction stories do.) Further, some of these stories have been previously collected: "Elsewhen" in *Far and Away*; "The Compleat Werewolf" and "The Pink Caterpillar" in *"The Compleat Werewolf" and Other Stories of Fantasy and Science Fiction* (Boucher's second book of short stories, 1969); and "The Ultimate Clue" in *Exeunt Murderers*.

With four of the seven stories previously collected, this volume might have problems selling. (Not everyone is as fanatical as I am about having collections of stories summing up a detective's career on his or her shelf.) I think the logical thing to do is to add "The Clue of the Knave of Diamonds" as a first "story" to the volume; it would give it a solid basis as detective fiction. Then the two novelettes, four short stories, and one short short would give the rest of O'Breen's non-novelistic cases, ending with that perfect climactic story, "The Ultimate Clue" (as *Exeunt Murderers* ends its collection of fiction, also). This would give a volume the size of about two novels bound together, not at all a bad size for an omnibus.

With the addition of "The Clue of the Knave of Diamonds," *perhaps* a standard detective-fiction publisher, such as The Mysterious Press, would consider this volume. Or perhaps one of the science-fiction specialty houses might do it, both for the sake of Boucher's name and for the reputation of "The Compleat Werewolf." And the volume could be advertised in two markets. (It would be one of the few volumes in which a private eye encounters a werewolf, a time machine, and an extraterrestrial--among other cases.)

CONUNDRUMS FOR A NUN

With his mystery writing established as by Anthony Boucher--Boucher's actual name, as most of my readers know, was William Anthony Parker White--Boucher developed a second pen name and a new detective. This was not unusual at the time: one thinks of Ellery Queen and Barnaby Ross, with their detectives Ellery Queen and Drury Lane; of John Dickson Carr and Carter Dickson, with Dr. Gideon Fell and Sir Henry Merrivale--and I assume the same economic motive today of producing more novels than one publisher can accept from one writer is behind, for example, Charlotte MacLeod and Alisa Craig, with Peter Shandy and Sarah Kelling Bitterson (separate series from MacLeod) and Detective Inspector Madoc Rhys, R.C.M.P. (from Craig).

As H.H. Holmes, Boucher produced two novels about Sister Ursula of the fictional Order of Martha of Bethany:
Nine Times Nine (1940)
Rocket to the Morgue (1942)
After his shift to magazine writing, Boucher produced two short

stories and a novella about her:
"Coffin Corner" (1943)
"The Stripper" (1945)
"Vacancy with Corpse" (1946)
The first two, the short stories, have been collected in *Exeunt Murderers*, so no new volume such as I'm proposing need be expected soon.   But sometime such a collection would be wonderful--particularly for gathering the never-reprinted novella.

Here again, since our current omnibuses often contain three novels, there seems to be no reason for all of the Sister Ursula accounts not to be included.   The only bibliographic addition I know of is the "Afterword" which appeared in a 1952 paperback edition of *Rocket to the Morgue*, discussing its sources.   And, of course, since the H.H. Holmes pseudonym is nearly forgotten, the omnibus should appear under the Boucher name, as did the later paperback editions of the novels.

What should this collection be called?   I titled the Sister Ursula section in the old bibliography "The Pride of Sister Ursula," but that echo of Father Brown only applies to a psychological struggle in the two novels, so it is misleading. One of the editors of *Exeunt Murderers* (again, probably Nevins) calls the two-story section "Conundrums for the Cloister," which has a nice alliteration.   I would prefer to go for the echo of the *nun* syllable and use either *Nun's Conundrums* or *Conundrums for a Nun*.   I used the latter for this section title only because the first is slightly more likely to be misread as a discussion of a modern nun's decision whether or not to fight for the ordination of women, or some other current problem of the sisters.   (A publisher probably would insist on some flat title like *Five Cases for Sister Ursula*. Maybe he or she could be convinced to use it as a subtitle to *Nun's Conundrums*.)

Although logically I do not think this volume is likely to appear soon, with two stories currently available, I should point out that this is my first suggestion which consists of pure detective stories.   It should have an appeal, if one considers the present popularity of such religious detective series as William X. Kienzle's novels about Father Robert Koesler.

MYSTERIOUS CALIFORNIA

At this point, I shift my emphasis away from Boucher's detectives.   I sometimes have wondered about how Boucher's other mysteries might be collected, and it has occurred to me that Boucher's love of his native state is well represented in his fiction.   He was fond of Hamlet's lines about actors, meaning, I suppose, their dramas, being "the abstract and brief chronicles of the time" (Act II, scene 2).   (Hamlet repeats the idea later, saying that the goal of drama is to show "the very age and body of the time his form and pressure"--Act III, scene 2.) However well the Elizabethan and Jacobean dramas reflect their period, it is certainly true that detective fiction often does this well: one thinks of the Victorian and Edwardian London of Sherlock Holmes and the late-twenties San Francisco of Sam

Spade. Boucher, also, although I won't argue the details here, often reflects his milieux.

Let me start with a list of Boucher's non-series mystery stories. Science-fictional mysteries are not included; neither are two pastiches (one each of Arsene Lupin and Sherlock Holmes), a historical mystery (about Jack the Ripper), and two "photo-crimes." This list, in short, indicates what one usually means by the term "mystery"; some are puzzles, some are not—or not entirely. When stories have appeared under more than one title, all titles are included, in their order of appearance. All but "Transcontinental Alibi" are collected in *Exeunt Murderers.*

> "Threnody"/"Death Can Be Beautiful" (written 1936, published 1952)
> "Design for Dying" (1941)
> "Mystery for Christmas" (1943)
> "Code Zed" (1944)
> "The Ghost with a Gun"/"Trick or Treat" (1945)
> "The Catalyst"/"The Numbers Man" (1945)
> "The Retired Hangman"/"Murder Was Their Business"/
> "You Can Get Used to Anything" (1947)
> "The Smoke-Filled Locked Room" (written c. 1950, published 1968)
> "Transcontinental Alibi" (1950)
> "A Matter of Scholarship" (1955)
> "The Statement of Jerry Malloy"/"Command Performance" (1955)

Of these, I find no locale other than an American urban background in "Code Zed," a World War II spy story; "Threnody" has an urban background also (a reference to night school and a long drive to the city's edge)—but nothing else, except the elimination of Hollywood, where the protagonist is planning to move.

What I was curious about was whether one could arrange the remaining stories by the California towns in which they are set: would a regional publisher in California find enough of a survey of the state to be interested in producing a small book of Boucher's stories? I have added a Martin Lamb story, "The Anomaly of the Empty Man," in order to have a San Francisco setting. Here is what I discovered, arranged from northern California to southern:

> SACRAMENTO
> "The Smoked-Filled Locked Room:
> BERKELEY
> "The Ghost with the Gun"
> "The Catalyst"
> "Transcontinental Alibi"
> ("A Matter of Scholarship")
> SAN FRANCISCO
> "The Anomaly of the Empty Man"
> PASADENA
> "The Retired Hangman"
> HOLLYWOOD (AND LAUREL CANYON)
> "Mystery for Christmas"
> "The Statement of Jerry Malloy"

LOS ANGELES
("Design for Dying")
I have put two of these stories in parenthesis, as not of probable interest to my hypothesized California publisher.

The events in "A Matter of Scholarship" occur in "Wortley Hall" on the campus of "the University"; since Boucher lived in Berkeley, I assume that this is a reference to the University of California at Berkeley campus. However, when I wrote to that school to check it out, Marcelle D. Patterson, Student Affairs Officer, replied (in a letter of 11 March 1986) that the closest campus name to Wortley Hall was Wurster Hall. (Wurster is near the southeast corner of the campus, not far from the International House which figured in *The Case of the Seven of Calvary*—if the latter has not shifted through the years.) This sounded all right, but I wondered whether Boucher had some other allusion in mind—a different university, or some private joke? I wrote to Phyllis White, Boucher's widow, who replied on 2 April 1986:

> The equivalent at U.C. of Wortley Hall at the un-named university would have been Wheeler. Wurster is out on two counts. It wasn't built until long after and it houses the College of Environmental Design. If there was some reason for selecting the name Wortley I don't know about it.

(Wheeler is just about in the center of the campus now, but, as Mrs. White commented in a later letter, "it wasn't then. It was the first building encountered after one entered by Sather Gate, of *Seven of Calvary* fame, on the south border" [letter of 20 June 1986].) I'm happy that Mrs. White implicitly shares my assumption that the school referred to in the story is U.C.-Berkeley; but I did not end up with a very satisfactory conclusion to this attempt at identification so far as my imaginary volume is concerned. A publisher would probably feel that this misnamed hall at an unnamed school was not clearly enough in California for the story to be collected.

On the other hand, "Design for Dying" *certainly* is laid in Los Angeles—but an average reader would not understand why. Lieutenant Herman Finch, L.A.P.D., appears in Boucher's novel *The Case of the Baker Street Irregulars* (1940); the only indication of locale in "Design for Dying" is that Finch is in charge of the murder investigation. (Finch also appears in two of the Nick Noble stories.) Since the evidence of locale is lacking for the reader who doesn't know Boucher's other fiction, a publisher probably would drop this tale. There is no local color in the story, obviously.

I must admit that there is one of these unparenthesized stories I have never seen—"Transcontinental Alibi." I wrote to Bob Briney about it, and he identified its locale at Berkeley, quoting from the story that its action moves "from the select residential district of Piedmont to the heights of the Berkeley hills" (letter of 17 March 1986). I had guessed the *transcontinental* referred to some sort of travel (train, bus, plane?);

but Bob informs me that "the term refers to the use of a transcontinental radio program (a quiz show) as part of an alibi for
murder." He adds that the story is a short-short, told from the
murderer's viewpoint. Since this story is not available to most
of us, I hope this filling out of information is an agreeable
digression.

I don't think there is much of bibliographic note to add to
this collection. *Exeunt Murderers* picks up Boucher's introduction for the M.W.A. anthology *Crime for Two*, edited by Frances
and Richard Lockridge (1955), which I hope this subsequent,
hypothesized collection would pick up also. I have mentioned
the preface to "The Anomaly of the Empty Man" above. If I
remember correctly, in that *Crime for Two* anthology (I haven't
seen the original magazine publication in E.Q.M.M.), the story
within the story in "Mystery for Christmas" was reproduced in
typewritten script, instead of *Exeunt Murderer's* standard type.
Since Ed McBain has been able to reproduce all sorts of police
forms, and other printed materials, in his 87th Precinct novels,
I see no reason why the typescript should not be reproduced in
this California collection. (Perhaps someone should check the
original publication of Boucher's stories to see, of course, if my
memory is right about "Mystery for Christmas" but also to see if
there are any other tales which Boucher thought would be
helped by reproduced items of various sorts--what about the
several supposedly typewritten notes which appear in the Nick
Noble story "Crime Must Have a Stop"?)

Let me add a geographic comment about my list of stories.
I know that Hollywood does not exist as a separate legal entity;
it has been part of Los Angeles since 1910. But the two stories
I have listed under the "Hollywood" designation refer to their
setting as Hollywood, and in the popular mind Hollywood *does*
exist. There is no reason to be pedantic in a collection of
popular literature. (I *will* be pedantic enough to mention, as my
list vaguely suggests, that in "Mystery for Christmas" the frame
is set in Hollywood; the inset story is placed in Laurel Canyon.)

Probably this book will not be published any time soon,
since only two of the eight (unparenthesized) stories do not
appear in *Exeunt Murderers* (and it took the addition of a
Martin Lamb story to get the number up to two). But it's the
sort of volume that might well appeal to a small regional press.
Eight short stories--or short short, in the case of "Transcontinental Alibi"--might well be part of the financial appeals.
A small book from a small publisher.

On the other hand, if a larger sort of omnibus is wanted,
there are two novels which might be included. I have already
mentioned *The Case of the Baker Street Irregulars*, a mystery
laid in Hollywood about the making of a Sherlock Holmes movie.
(If this book were included, then "Design for Dying" might be
included, since Finch's context would be introduced.) The other
novel is *The Marble Forest* (1951), published under the pseudonym of Theo Durrant and written by Boucher and eleven other
members of the California branch of the M.W.A. It is laid in
"Red Forks," which I take to be an invented town name; it has
to be in northern California since it is a short bus ride from

Sacramento. (I assume the name is made up because I don't find a California town called that in *The World Almanac.* Maybe the name is meant to suggest the redwood trees of the area.)

Here, then, is the fuller version of this California collection:

"RED FORKS" (Northern California)
   The Marble Forest (collaboration, 1953)
SACRAMENTO
   "The Smoke-Filled Locked Room" (written c. 1950)
BERKELEY
   "The Ghost with the Gun" (1945)
   "The Catalyst" (1945)
   "Transcontinental Alibi (1950)
SAN FRANCISCO
   "The Anomaly of the Empty Man" (1952)
PASADENA
   "The Retired Hangman" (1947)
LOS ANGELES (Hollywood, Laurel Canyon, etc.)
   The Case of the Baker Street Irregulars (1940)
   "Design for Dying" (1941)
   "Mystery for Christmas" (1943)
   "The Statement of Jerry Malloy" (1955)

I have left the framework of the state towns since I assume they would be retained on the contents page of this collection—simply for clarification of the reader's (and, earlier, purchaser's) expectations.

Whether in the longer or the shorter form, I think the basic idea of a California collection of Boucher's stories is good: he was, after all, in and through his genre fiction, a regional writer.

CONCLUSION

All too often publishers seem very uncreative about what they reprint. I can think of several omnibuses which pick very odd groups of three (or so) novels to represent an author's works. Sometimes, indeed, I suspect omnibuses are based on whatever novels happen to be not currently in paperback, or whatever novels' rights can be picked up most cheaply, nothing else. (As all mystery readers know, occasionally there are very good reasons why a novel by a name author has not been reprinted and why it is available cheaply!)

Whether or not my above suggestions ever find their way into print. I believe that they show a bit more concern with thematic or protagonistic unity than do some collections. I should add that I offer these suggestions freely: I do not expect to receive either money or recognition if, say, the California volume is published. Or if any of them are. But it would be nice if the publisher would send me a free copy of the book.

The Cream of Queen

Frank Floyd

MARCH-APRIL

Peter Turnbull. "McNaught's Obsession." April, 1987.

April brings "The Theft of the Lost Slipper," one of Edward D. Hoch's stories about Nick Velvet. These stories are clue-given; the "Lost Slipper" is a clue. The first step in solving is the discovery of the crime, and of the remaining steps the most important is learning why the clue is a clue.

In "McNaught's Obsession" Peter Turnbull tells an emotional tale about what happens as a result of Torfin ("a Gaelic name, very common on the Orkney Islands and the Shetlands as well") McNaught's obsessive, one-sided infatuation with Sandra McAuley, a young woman who—we find out when the Glasgow police investigate her poignant death—is not interested in him. "McNaught's Obsession" is a hard-nosed police procedural with plenty of atmosphere and realism—it is basic police work with no tricks and no cute writing. By the end we know something of Glasgow, which "is the most Victorian city in Great Britain, if not Europe, if not the world," and the Glaswegians, and we know much more about the victim, the murderer, and the several policemen who share the investigative duties.

The story owes much of its appeal to its reliable solidity and trustworthiness. Turnbull is on the side of the Glasgow police. The police are on the side of the victim. The murderer is himself responsible for his murdering a harmless young woman. Working as it is supposed to do, the system is not to blame.

As part of the system, the Glasgow police department carries out its function commendably.

Further Gems from the Literature

William F. Deeck

The defendant's chance, it would appear, are slim and dim:

... In the ensuing silence a plaintiff voice came from the bench....--*The Eye of Osiris*, by R. Austin Freeman.

Department of felicitous remarks:

"That," said Tyler solemnly, "is a moot point and one on which the Supreme Court would have to sit...."--*Murder in the State Department*, by Diplomat.

"Damn!" snarled Dover, for whom work was a four-letter word.--"Dover Weighs the Evidence," by Joyce Porter.

Department of anticlimax:

First it made him furiously angry, then apoplectic, then diabolically insane with rage, and for the last quarter of an hour it affected his stomach.--*Vampire of the Skies*, by James Corbett.

Oh, it was, was it?

"It was Dupin who said that when you have eliminated the impossible, then whatever remains however improbable must be true."--*Through a Glass Darkly*, by Val Gielgud.

How's-that-again? department:

From the passage outside he heard a dull plop. That sound could never be mistaken. It came from a silenced revolver.--

Heads You Live, by David Hume.

His face turned a livid red....--*The Victim Was Important*, by Joe Rayter.

Home-cooked food was a tantalizing bait after our alfresco meals in the office.--*Said with Flowers*, by Anne Nash.

"I couldn't go to sleep last night for thinking there was something bigger involved, something of which we haven't got the faintest inkling yet. When I woke up this morning I was more convinced of it than ever."--*The Midnight Mail*, by Henry Holt.

It was like looking for an ostrich in a forest of monkeys!--*Vampire of the Skies*, by James Corbett.

Neatest tricks of the week:

The boy cringed against the wall and falsetto animal noises came out through his nose.--*One Angel Less*, by H.W. Roden.

One of her satin mules dropped off and Hayes saw her bare toes, the nails painted scarlet, the ankle slack with astonishment.--*The Shivering Bough*, by Noel Burke.

She was pouring all her attention down the dark funnel of onrushing road....--*If a Body*, by George Worthing Yates.

About him, the maple-wood furniture of suite seven stood shivering in the chill of a December morning.--*Seven Keys to Baldpate*, by Earl Derr Biggers.

Mr. Tuttle's little black eyes shot venom.--*Dog Eat Dog*, by Mary Collins.

Her eyes were literally boring hateful holes into me.--*Three Short Biers*, by Jimmy Starr.

Neatest neatest trick of the week:

Not a wrinkle in his neat clothes was out of place....--*The Mad Hatter Mystery*, by John Dickson Carr.

Promises, promises:

"I am not going to worry you with questions, Miss Tabitha, but I have come along to ask you what has happened? Can you tell me in a few words? It think there is something on your mind you would like to tell me personally? You can trust me, can't you?"--*The Merrivale Mystery*, by James Corbett.

Hisses one doubts ever got hissed:

"Mildred Clay!" he hissed.--*Wedding Treasure*, by David Williams.

I hissed at her under my breath. "Anne! Don't you dare unlock that door! Anne!"--*A Party for the Shooting*, by Louisa Revell.

"I didn't hear anything," I protested in a hiss.--*Strangled Prose*, by Joan Hess.

"Next time your boy won't be in the other room," he hissed.--*The Victim Was Important*, by Joe Rayter.

... She snatched them back, hissing: "Get out of the way. Leave me alone!"--*A Touch of Stagefright*, by Jocelyn Davey.

Has Barzun been told the sad news?

With due respect to the late William S. Baring Gould [sic], the late Bernard DeVoto, the late professor Jacques Barzun....--*The Brownstone House of Nero Wolfe*, by Ken Darby.

Five-card-stud poker as played by Johnny Fletcher and Sam Cragg, or no wonder they're always broke:

"I raise it two hundred," said Chatsworth. He had a five showing.... Sam dealt another round of cards. Chatsworth paired up his five that had been showing.... Sam dealt the fourth card, an ace to Chatsworth.... The last card came around. Chatsworth matched up his five ... which made it look like three fives, since he had raised on his first five.--*The Honest Dealer*, by Frank Gruber.

It's About Crime

Marvin Lachman

Although mystery fiction has had more than its share of characters with psychiatric conditions, there have been few books set in psychiatric institutions. Coincidentally, two of these are currently available in paperback, and they are both worth seeking out. *A Mind to Murder* (1963; reprinted by Warner Books, $3.50) is P.D. James's second novel and draws heavily on her own experience for its setting, a London psychiatric outpatient clinic. The victim is a hospital administrator, a position Miss James held in the British Civil Service System. Not only does the author know the workings of such a clinic, but she also knows the heartbreak of mental illness firsthand, since her husband, a physician, was hospitalized due to that condition for most of the twenty years before his death in 1964. Authenticity is the strong point of this book, along with the writing, which is civilized and perceptive; its plotting is adequate, but it is not as good in that regard as the 1962 James debut novel, *Cover Her Face.*

James is very adept at characterization, especially as regards Adam Dalgliesh, her series detective, who shows depths not often found in sleuths who solve the kind of classic puzzles James presents. Her skillful writing evokes considerable poignancy in describing his personal life. There is also a superbly written section about his searching the apartment of the victim, and Dalgliesh has enough empathy to realize that the necessary act is a violation of a dead person. If P.D. James seems to have received an inordinate amount of praise in recent years, do not begrudge it to her. She, more than most, combines the ability to plot interesting puzzles with the writing skill to observe society, create real characters, and write with intelligence and sophistication.

During the nineteen-thirties many movie comedies had the hero and heroine meet "cute." Example: Claudette Colbert and Gary Cooper meeting in a haberdashery; he only wants pajama bottoms, and she only wants pajama tops. They agree to buy a single pair. Patrick Quentin's *A Puzzle for Fools* (1936) is in that tradition, as Peter Duluth, an alcoholic theatrical producer, and Iris Pattison, a young woman suffering from melancholia, met at an exclusive mental sanatorium. This book has seldom been out of print since it was first published more than fifty years ago, and it has now been reprinted in trade paperback by Penguin ($5.95) to launch a new Classic Crime series.

The Duluth books were to get better as time went on. This book, the first which Hugh C. Wheeler and Richard Wilson Webb wrote as Patrick Quentin, is lively and readable but shows some of the earmarks of inexperience (Wheeler was only twenty-four at the time) and hasty writing; the team was very prolific in the years before World War II. Duluth's fears as he goes through alcohol withdrawal while trying to solve a murder are not well conveyed. Instead, we have him saying things like, "Those were some of the most harrowing moments of my life," but the authors do not make the readers feel it. Too often the authors rely on Had-I-But-Known writing to get across that there are sinister events to come. For example: "Of course, I had no idea then of the fantastic and horrible things which were soon to happen in Doctor Lenz's sanatorium. I had no means of telling just how significant these minor and seemingly pointless disturbances were." And, later, "Maybe I could have prevented a lot of tragedy if I had gone to the authorities there and then." (Quentin comes close to setting a world's record for the amount of information withheld from the police in this book.)

The pace is very quick, and Duluth's light, self-deprecating tone makes him an enjoyable narrator. Don't expect the kind of sophistication to be found in the British puzzles of the nine-teen-thirties, though Wheeler and Webb were born in England. No American writer has quite achieved what is to be found in Allingham, Innes, Blake, Sayers, et al. There must be an invisible barrier on the western shore of the Atlantic. Incidentally, if the name Hugh Wheeler sounds familiar, it should. After he stopped writing mysteries in 1965 he became a major playwright, best known for his collaborations with Stephen Sondheim on such works as *A Little Night Music, Pacific Overtures,* and *Sweeney Todd.*

The British are not immune to soap opera, but they do seem to write it better than we do. A case in point is *New Year Resolution* by Alison Cairns (St. Martin's, $12.95), which I appropriately started on January first. Cairns tells of broken marriages, infidelity, unmarried mothers, deserted children, drugs, drink, other forms of unhappiness, and murder. However, she writes well and takes a large cast of characters and makes each distinctive. As a result, I cared about them and overcame the repugnance with which I usually greet television "soaps." *Warning:* The dust jacket may be dangerous to your reading enjoyment. It hints broadly at the identity of the murder victim, even though that person is not dispatched until page 148 of the 203 page book.

Harper's Perennial Library keeps reprinting Dorothy L. Sayers, proving that there will always be an audience for class. In her lifetime Sayers published eleven Lord Peter Wimsey novels and three short story collections which included Wimsey stories. Perennial has now republished nine of the novels and all of the short story collections in uniform paperback editions at $3.95 each. (I suspect that the two remaining novels, *The*

Unpleasantness at the Bellona Club and *The Nine Tailors*, will also be reprinted shortly.)   In addition, there is a trade paperback of almost five hundred pages, *Lord Peter* ($8.95), which contains *all* of the Wimsey short stories, including three that were never previously published in book collections. That book is enhanced by a James Sandoe introduction, an essay by Carolyn Heilbrun (who writes mysteries as Amanda Cross), and a delicious Wimsey parody, "Greedy Night," by E.C. Bentley. Speaking of bonuses, I must again praise the illustration By Marie Michal which appears on all of the covers. They're some of the best done paperback art I've seen in years.

I'm not sure if there's anything else about Sayers that hasn't already been said. I could suggest that her non-series short stories not be overlooked since they are uncommonly good, especially "The Man Who Knew How," in *Hangman's Holiday*, as well as "Suspicion" and "The Leopard Lady," in *In the Teeth of the Evidence*. Those volumes also contain stories about Sayer's other series detective, wine salesman Montague Egg. Very down to earth with his advice on how salesmen should succeed, his stories are "no-nonsense," yet imaginative in plotting.   I especially enjoyed his information about wine.   I would also suggest that one not be put off by the foppish quality of Lord Peter. I'm not sure why some detectives between the wars, like Wimsey, Reginald Fortune, and the early Albert Campion, were created as silly asses. The fact is that, if given half a chance, they will prove that they are far from effete.   Also, their authors, especially Sayers, are people of intelligence, and they write as if they assume the same about their readers.   These days, one feels that many writers are appealing mainly to our emotions or our libidos.

As promised in a previous column, I have continued to delve into the fascinating story of King Richard III and whether he was responsible for the murder of his young nephews, the Princes, in the Tower of London. As you'll recall, we had the Richardist viewpoint as set forth by Tey in her justly famous novel, *The Daughter of Time*, which exonerated him, and the traditional position which Guy Townsend successfully worked into the plot of his first mystery, *To Prove a Villain*.   The problem is that there are so few contemporary accounts from five hundred years ago, so we don't know who is right.

Audrey Williamson won a CWA God Dagger Award with *The Mystery of the Princes: An Investigation into a Supposed Murder* (1978), which has now been printed in this country in a well illustrated trade paperback edition by Academy Chicago Publishers ($8.95). Her title gives her point of view; she is clearly Richardist and often uses sources as they suit her.   For example, the accounts of Mancini, which come as close to being contemporary as anyone's, are used when Williamson finds them helpful but downplayed at other times. I note that she ignored Townsend's scholarly article on this matter in *The Armchair Detective*; I guess fan magazines have not achieved enough respectability yet.   Still, Williamson's book can be highly recommended because, even if she hasn't read Townsend, she has read widely, and she does a masterful job of presenting a large group of characters and complex events in very clear terms. Whether historians should find fault with this book, I cannot say. However, it is definitely recommended for educated lay people who are interested in this still unresolved case.

For what it's worth, having read Tey, Townsend, and Williamson, I am still not certain of the truth in the matter. I am sure that were I sitting on a jury trying Richard III right now, I would vote for acquittal since there is virtually no factual evidence to find him guilty. I believe Henry VII had more of a motive than Richard to eliminate the Princes since they were more of a threat to *his* succession. After all, Parliament had already acceded to Richard and provided a bar sinister by finding the princes to be bastards as a result of Edward IV's marriage to Eleanor Butler prior to his marrying Elizabeth Woodville, their mother. Many of the accounts written after Henry VII took the throne, e.g., that of Sir Thomas More, appear to have altered the facts to curry favor with the Tudors.

I also find Richard III's historical and psychological profile inconsistent with the murder of helpless children. He was loyal to his brother, Edward IV, and unlikely to kill his brother's children. He was eventually accepted by the mother and sister of the Princes, and the evidence indicates this was as much due to his generosity as due to their fear of him. He was generous to survivors, even of those he put to death, e.g., Lord Hastings, regardless of whether one accepts the equivocal evidence that he had Hastings killed the same day he was arrested. Finally, Richard III was a king who was responsible for progressive laws, and he died bravely at Bosworth, though he probably never said "My kingdom for a horse!" On the other hand, the more devious Henry VII was safely in the back lines while this crucial battle was going on.

One of the last mysteries published in 1986, *The 120-Hour Clock* by Francis M. Nevins, Jr. (Walker hardcover, $15.95), turned out to be one of the most enjoyable. Nevins has abandoned (except for a cameo appearance) his previous series sleuth, Loren Mensing, in favor of an extraordinary con man, Milo Turner, whose life and happiness depend upon his solving a murder. The first chapter is an absolute grabber, beginning with a paragraph from Turner's notebook in which he sounds the way Cornell Woolrich might have if he were reflecting on his career as a con man, instead of as a writer. After that we ride the Milonic roller coaster, mostly through New York and St. Louis, a world which includes Schultz's Human Supermarket and Lafferty's Identity Bazaar.

Nevins operates on two levels. First, his book is a big-caper novel and practically a treatise on the scam, though its pace is far from scholarly. Using verbs the way Nevins does (purists may blanche), I can say I page-turned compulsively. Yet Nevins evokes considerable poignancy from his character, and, incidentally, he writes excellent love scenes, several with a nicely erotic touch. If you've heard that Walker only publishes "cozy" books, disenchant yourself of that notion. The sex and the language are strong here, but they are appropriate; nothing is gratuitous.

The mystery reader of the future, say in the twenty-second century, can learn a great deal about how we lived in the latter half of this century from *The 120-Hour Clock*. There are scenes in large motels that perfectly capture how it is to spend time there. In another scene, Turner and a woman he loves walk through Manhattan: "I linked my arm in hers as we trod the empty streets, talking in whispers so we wouldn't wake the bag people sleeping on the steam vents." I'm not sure I believe all of this book, especially the ease with which Turner establishes new identities. I'm not ever sure I was supposed to. After all, Nevins is really in the same field as Turner, who says he's "in the business of giving apparent reality to what doesn't exist." Both are highly successful at their professions.

I'm on record as having serious reservations about occult and horror fiction, feeling most works in those genres are "cop-outs" in which the authors do not play by the "rules" of reality. Jon L. Breen's *The Gathering Place* (1984; reprinted in paperback by Walker, $2.95) contains one unexplainable element, the ability of its heroine, Rachel Hennings, to, without practice, imitate the signatures of famous authors like Erle Stanley Gardner. The plot device of automatic writing doesn't help what is otherwise a classic detective story, but it doesn't hurt it enough to keep me from recommending this book. The setting is a famous old bookstore on Santa Monica Boulevard in Los Angeles, recently inherited by Hennings from her uncle. There is real murder to go with the supernatural, and soon Rachel is acting as detective, with some help from a psychology professor, a reporter, and a Los Angeles Police detective. Hennings is a strong enough character that she probably doesn't need that many extra detectives. The mystery is crisply told and satisfactorily resolved, by strictly logical means. A real bonus is the atmosphere of an old-fashioned book store as seen through the eyes of an author who obviously loves old books.

Atmosphere is always a strong element in any John Dickson Carr novel, and that is true of *Panic in Box C* (1966), one of the last of his Gideon Fell series, reprinted by Carroll and Graf in paper for $3.50. By the time he wrote this book, Carr was long settled in the United States, the place of his birth, and increasingly he was finding reasons for Fell to travel and detect here. This time Fell is on a lecture tour, but he detours to attend a performance of *Romeo and Juliet* in Westchester County. Not only is there the obligatory murder and elements of impossible crime, but there is also effective use of the theatre, both its physical settings and its lore, to add to an unusually good detective story. Fell remains one of my favorite detectives, a wonderfully eccentric Chestertonian type whose bluster artfully conceals his marvelous brain. His solution is one of the best and most witty in a long career of brilliant explanations by Carr.

A recent sub-genre of the mystery is the historical set in the *recent* past, not a century or more ago as were some of the non-series books of John Dickson Carr. Foremost exponents of this new sub-genre, which features actual people, are Andrew

Bergman and Stuart Kaminsky, but there are others, including,
now, Stephen Wright, who makes his debut with *The Adventures
of Sandy West, Private Eye* (available in a large size paperback
edition from Mystery Notebook Editions, P.O. Box 1341, F.D.R.
Station, New York, NY   10150, $9.50 plus $2.00 for postage,
packing, and insurance).   Try to imagine a mystery in which
Dashiell Hammett, W. Somerset Maugham, Marilyn Monroe, and
Humphrey Bogart play important roles.   Since Sandy West is
probably mystery fiction's first bisexual detective, part of the
suspense comes from trying to guess who's going to bed with
whom.

A combination of serious murder mystery and spoof of this
sub-genre, it doesn't really succeed as either but will entertain
the reader willing to suspend disbelief, enjoy very erotic
passages, and have some fun following the adventures of a very
inexperienced detective who meets Dashiell Hammett on a train
to New York immediately after World War II.   West is returning
after being discharged from the U.S. Navy; Hammett is heading
East to open a detective agency in New York, and he hires
West.   Soon West is on his first case and traveling around New
York, and then Hollywood, in famous company to solve it.
Because the author, like his hero, is relatively inexperienced,
there are not enough real clues or detection to make this book
appeal to lovers of classic detection. Also, there is occasional
repetitiveness.   Sandy West drinks enough Scotch during the
book to float the British Navy (and fill several pages). Still, he
is different from any other private eye I've read about, and it
isn't often that one can say that about a character.

No series on TV has so consistently appealed to real
mystery fans as *Mystery!* on PBS, and the rerelease of the books
on which the series is based has been a bonus.   A Two-part
presentation of *The Secret Adversary* (1922) was an improvement
over the Tommy and Tuppence short stories that had been on
the show in past years.   The stories, collected in *Partners in
Crime*, were intended as parody/pastiches and, as such, were
better suited to reading than watching. On the other hand, *The
Secret Adversary*, which recounts the meeting of the young
couple, is an exciting thriller with plenty of action, ideally
suited for the screen. Whether or not you saw it on television,
I can recommend the book, republished in its twenty-fourth (!)
printing by Bantam, for $3.50.   Read this or *N or M* and see
how good Christie was in her earlier days writing about the
Beresfords--and then contrast it with *Posterns of Fate*, an
embarrassing late book published after she should have retired.

As I write this, *Mystery!* is in the midst of another series
of Sherlock Holmes tales, and these have been collected by
Penguin as *The Return of Sherlock Holmes*, for $3.50.   No, this
is not the original 1904 collection under that title, which
contained thirteen stories, but it does contain all seven stories
of the current series, and they are among Doyle's best, including such gems as the Adventures of "The Empty House," "The
Musgrave Ritual," and "The Abbey Grange."   If your life has
been deprived until now, there is no better time than this year
(the one-hundredth anniversary of the first Holmes story) to

start reading about the Great Man, and this is a good collection with which to begin.

Due on *Mystery!* in the near future is an adaptation of P.D. James's first mystery novel, *Cover Her Face*, which I reviewed so favorably in my last column. The book has been published by Warner for $3.50.

Grounds for Murder
a mystery book store
Old Town Mercado,   2707 Congress St.,   San Diego, CA 92110   (619) 294-9497

Dear Friends in Mystery,

The San Diego Bouchercon 19 Committee is pleased to announce that Charlotte MacLeod has accepted our invitation to be the guest of honor at the 1988 Bouchercon in San Diego.

Our toastmaster, fan guest of honor, any special visiting guests, and other honorees will be announced over the coming months.

We are attempting to compile a complete list of all living mystery writers and their addresses so that no one will be left off the invitation list. We are asking all chapters of MWA to send us their membership mailing lists. If any writer of "criminous fiction" (or related material) reading this letter is not a member of MWA or has mystery author friends who are not members, please assist us by sending us your name and address and/or asking your friends to do so.

We have already begun work on setting up our panels and other program. We would welcome any suggestions and ideas you may wish to offer for program or for the general running of the Bouchercon. (Obviously, we will not be able to use all the suggestions we receive, but we will welcome them and give them our consideration.)

We are currently accepting advance memberships for the 1988 Bouchercon. If paid more than a year in advance, the cost of a membership is $25.00. After that it will probably go up to $30.00, and then $35.00 at the door.

We look forward to hearing from you and receiving your suggestions.

Yours truly in crime,

Ray Hardy

R H

Phyllis Brown

Co-chairpersons of the
Bouchercon 19 Committee

Reel Murders
(Movie Reviews)

Walter Albert

"Bob the Gambler"

One of the advantages of being something of a round peg
in a department of square holes is that I am occasionally
allowed to teach something that nobody else has any interest in
doing, like the course on French Film that I have just finished
teaching. Most of the films are by directors like Renoir, Clair,
Virgo, Carne, and Ophuls, but I always manage to slip in a
genre film by a director not many people would consider
essential.   In past years this meant films by Clouzot ("Le
Corbeau" and "Jenny Lamour").   This year it was Jean-Pierre
Melville's 1955 thriller, "Bob le flambeur [Bob the gambler]," a
film that Melville had repudiated before his death in 1972 ("I
will not allow this film ever to be screened again") but that
many critics now consider to be his finest achievement in a
series of studies of criminals and the criminal milieu.
Ostensibly, "Bob the Gambler" is an extended character
study leading to a climactic caper, the robbery, by a team of
well trained specialists, of the casino at Deauville. But Melville
manages to undermine almost every cliche of the caper film with
a rigorously analytic style that manages to distance the spectator from the characters and cut away from the caper at the
climactic moment, only returning to it in the final moments to
dispense almost briskly with the basic plot elements and provide
a final, comically ironic look at the protagonist, Bob the
gambler.
Melville, in an interview, related how, after seeing
Huston's film "The Asphalt Jungle," he realized that he no
longer wanted to--or could not--make a classic caper film. He
decided instead to make what he called a "comedy of manners"
("comedie de moeurs"), but most American viewers will probably,
like the students in my class, find this an odd film indeed.
Melville's film preceded New Wave films like Truffaut's
"The 400 Blows" and Godard's "Breathless" by about four years,
but the look of the film (shot on location in the streets and
buildings of Montmartre) and the use of a jazz sound track
seem to look forward to the innovative filmmaking of the late
fifties and early sixties. The credits are presented over shots
of Montmartre from the "heights" of Sacre-Coeur (the church)

to the "depths" of Place Pigalle, a moral distance underlined by
the matter-of-fact narration of Melville. But the spectator who
expects an explicit moralistic study of the contrasts between the
sacred and the profane will be disconcerted as the camera
prowls restlessly along the streets, into the back rooms of cafes
and restaurants, with Sacre-Coeur only present as a shape dimly
glimpsed through the closed curtains of Bob's elegant apartment.
The affection the camera shows for the landscape may be
disconcerting to the viewer who is looking for a narrative
thread that will engage him, but location filming is a prominent
feature of New Wave films, as in "The 400 Blows," whose
"travelogue" beginning is reminiscent of the beginning of "Bob,"
all the more so in that both films benefitted from the same
superb photographer, Henri Decae.

The final shot in "Bob" is of an empty car parked on a
lonely stretch of beach and completes a circle initiated by the
documentary shots of buildings at the beginning of the film.
The inner life of the characters is never explored in a way that
is satisfying to the viewer, and it is perhaps appropriate that
the frame is emptied of people at the beginning and the end.
The viewer expecting the tight plotting of Hitchcock or the
claustrophobic, fatalistic character study of Huston will be
disappointed. In Melville's work, fate is chance, but the camera
lingers on geometric patterns (wall-paper, windows, a floor
covering) that suggest an intercrossing of plot lines that will
only be evident on repeated viewings. The characters are
elusive and the "content" of their relationships is like a
crossword puzzle that may or may not be correctly filled in by
the spectator.

Melville's expressed wish that the film not be re-released
has been ignored. The formal, discreet patterns of this
apparently open but controlled narrative with something of the
look of a photograph by Walker Evans have lost none of their
capacity for frustrating the viewer accustomed to the height-
ened, mounting suspense of Huston's "The Asphalt Jungle" (1950)
or Kubrick's "The Killing" (1956). All three of these films are
about defeat and loss, but "Bob" manages to retrieve an ironic
victory from a failure, and the sardonic humor of this victory
appears to clash with the conventions it has intermittently
adhered to. In "Breathless," Goddard paid tribute to Melville by
including a reference to the character, Bob, and by using
Melville to play the role of a novelist interviewed by Patricia,
the young American with whom the small-time Parisian hoodlum,
Michel, has fallen in love. She betrays Michel, echoing the
thematics of betrayal in "Bob," where Anne betrays Paulo and
Bob's careful planning, but the final irony is perhaps Melville's
attempted betrayal of his beautiful and still fascinating portrait
of Bob the gambler and his Parisian milieu.

And one can only wonder to what extent Godard was again
tipping his hat to Melville when one of his characters comments
that he and his friends avoid Montmartre, which is dangerous
for them and their "kind." But Godard met successfully the
cinematic challenge of his gifted predecessor and his tribute is,
finally, the best witness to Melville's achievement.

Verdicts

(Book Reviews)

Richard L. Knudson.   *The Whole Spy Catalogue.*   St. Martin's,
1986, 182 pp., $10.95.

So you want to be a spy?

The Whole Spy Catalogue, a new handbook published
inexpensively in soft covers, is an invaluable reference for
anyone who has ever dreamed of going undercover.

It dissects the world of espionage from a number of angles.
In an introductory chapter we are reminded that "espionage
is nothing new. The Bible's Old Testament abounds with tales
of intrigue and stealth. Perhaps the first spy gadget was the
pair of scissors Delilah used to cut Sampson's hair in ca 1100
b.c. We can be assured that the business of spying is as old as
the separation of men into groups such as tribes or nations."

The historical survey of the second-oldest profession begins
with the rivalry of cavemen who must have sent spies to steal
the secret of fire; the mission of the scouts sent out by Moses
to the land of Canaan and their report that the Israelites were
headed for a land of milk and honey; and Joshua's instructions
to two undercover men, "Go view the land, even to Jericho."

An ancient book, "The Art of War," by the Chinese general
Sun Tzu, discusses cloak-and-dagger operations of twenty-five
hundred years ago. Victory, the general maintained, depends
upon foreknowledge, and he categorized various classes of secret
agents. His main advice was, "Be subtle! Be subtle!... Spies
are the most important element in war, because upon them
depends the army's ability to move."

The Roman Catholic Church established a highly organized
secret service under Pope Innocent III; its prime purpose was to
identify all enemies of the church.

In the 1500s, most of the major European nations instituted
formal intelligence forces. England's spy corps became very
adept at deciphering codes.

In America, George Washington created the first secret
service. Perhaps the most famous American spy of all time was
Nathan Hale, who was captured behind British lines during the
Revolutionary War when making sketches and taking notes. Just
before the noose was tightened around his neck, Hale said, "I
only regret that I have but one life to lose for my country."

Over the years, strong nations of the world have developed strong secret services. Today is no exception. America's CIA and Russia's KGB are the two espionage organizations against which all others are compared. England's MI5 and MI6 are also highly regarded, and some authorities claim that Israel's Mossad is the best in the world. States author Knudson: "In 1986, just as in 500 b.c., foreknowledge is very important. It is not only important in war but also in peace."

The Whole Spy Catalogue continues with some theories of ethical guidelines for the spy and offers tidbits of information as to how to apply for a job with the CIA. The secret service organizations, responsible for espionage and counterespionage, of many countries are listed alphabetically. Interestingly, SMERSH is not just a fancy enterprise created by Ian Fleming for the James Bond books, but is an actual Russian branch of the KGB (its name is based on the translation "death to spies"). A chapter dedicated to "Spies on the Shelf" deals with the realm of intelligence literature, both fiction and nonfiction. Richard Knudson believes that "most of the outstanding spy writers such as (Charles) McCarry, (Ian) Fleming, and (John) Le Carre have experience in espionage." This theory belies the phenomenal success of Tom Clancy, author of The Hunt for Red October (1985), the story of a Russian submarine, who had not been aboard a sub until well after the book became a best seller.

Knudson figures that the seeds of the spy novel were implanted in The Spy (1821) by James Fenimore Cooper and in "The Intelligence Office" (1844) by Nathaniel Hawthorne. He neglects to mention the fledgling pioneering efforts by Lord Lytton-Bulwer, Sir Walter Scott, and Robert Louis Stevenson.

Modern spy literature became established in 1903 with the British publication of The Riddle of the Sands by Erskine Childers, in which the plot centers on a young diplomat who discovers a German plan to invade England.

During this early period several authors, including William Le Queux, John Buchan, and E. Philips Oppenheim, helped to popularize fiercely patriotic spy stories. By the outbreak of World War II, the genre was firmly established as the single most common kind of fiction being published.

W. Somerset Maugham gave a boost to spy literature when he wrote Ashenden, or, The British Agent (1928), and Eric Ambler took espionage from the rich, brave, sophisticated hero and realistically demonstrated that spying was done by ordinary people in everyday situations.

The Whole Spy Catalogue lists many of the important contributors to the genre, including a few prolific authors who penned mostly paperback originals (Edward S. Aarons and Donald Hamilton are checklisted; Philip Atlee, Michael Avallone, Alan Cailou, and Stephen Marlowe are not).

Among Knudson's choices as prime innovators in the field are the British authors "Sapper" (a pseudonym of H.C. McNeile, who wrote ten books about the exploits of Hugh "Bulldog" Drummond, "a World War I hero who enlisted several of his Army mates to battle evil" [sort of an early "A-Team"]), Manning Coles (the penname of two writers who collaborated on a series of twenty-five international-intrigue yarns featuring Tommy Hambledon, a British Intelligence agent who "thoroughly enjoyed life and concentrated on living for the moment"), Len Deighton (who "has written some excellent spy novels which have solidified the form and added to its respect"), and Ian Fleming (who created fourteen adventures about James Bond, agent 007, who is licensed to kill). Also, Graham Greene (a mainstream novelist who wrote espionage "entertainments"), Adam Hall (penname of Elleston Trevor, creator of the Quiller cases about an agent who "possesses unusually deadly talents gained behind Nazi lines during World War II"), John Le Carre (whose *Spy Who Came in from the Cold* [1963] introduced George Smiley, "a spy and a hero in the way that only spies can be heroes--unknown, perhaps even to themselves"), and Peter O'Donnell (whose Modesty Blaise is "the best fictional female of note" and "combines sexy good looks with an extraordinary ability to cope with any adversary").

Among the American authors covered are John P. Marquand (who originated the mysterious Japanese agent, Mr. Moto), F. van Wyck Mason (whose series hero was Hugh North, the solver of murder mysteries rooted in international intrigue), Charles McCarry ("the best spy novelist today").

The glaring omissions from the list of notable espionage authors are John Creasey, Gavin Black, Brian Cleeve, Desmond Cory, and Simon Harvester.

Knudson offers some practical advice about how to launch a collection of cloak-and-dagger literature. He warns the would-be collector that a first edition of Ian Fleming's *Casino Royale* with dust jacket would sell today for more than $1,000, "but take heart, the American book club edition of the same book will sell for $10."

Included is a list of book dealers in the field who are apt to be able to help the novice collector.

A section titled "Spies on the Screen" is very sketchy, and the author's contention that "the invention of the talking motion picture did not do a great deal to elevate the spy film as an art" is debatable. The early vintage movies of Alfred Hitchcock, made in England during the 1930s, were excellent intrigue fare that have utilized dialogue and sound effects to great advantage.

The *Catalogue* highlights popular screen heroes James Bond, as portrayed by Sean Connery and Roger More, and Harry Palmer, the agent, played by Michael Caine, who was neither an officer nor a gentleman but got the job done in three successful movies.

Then there are concise descriptions of television's under-cover heroes Napoleon Solo (played by Robert Vaughn in *The Man from Uncle*), Agent 86, Maxwell Smart (played by Don Adams in *Get Smart*, who messes up his assignments in an irreverent spoof of the genre), Jim Phelps (played by Peter Graves in *Mission Impossible*), Kelly Robinson and Alexander Scott (played by Robert Culp and Bill Cosby in over seventy-five episodes of *I Spy*, a series that dealt mainly with cold-war issues), John Drake (the *Secret Agent* man, played by Patrick

36 Verdicts (Book Reviews)

McGoohan, who worked for World Travel, itself a cover for the British secret service), and John Steed (suave, brave, and quick-witted operator played by Patrick MacNee in *The Avengers*).

The Whole Spy Catalogue continues with "The Gadgetry of Spying," including a tiny device implanted under the skin of an agent so that he can be tracked anywhere on earth via satellite; "a very handy, quite complete and easy to use" set of lockpicks; assorted weapons like the Urban Shiv, "a strong, steel dagger designed for palm thrusts"; the Vantage, a hidden knife that also serves as a belt buckle; and the Wild Hair, a knife whose handle looks like the end of a comb.

Among other gadgets are the Attache Armor Pad, which provides ballistic protection from most handgun calibers, a paper shredder with strong steel teeth that turns the toughest paper into unreadable strips, and various electronic devices for eavesdropping, recording, transmitting, and photographing.

The indefatigable author also covers advanced weapon systems and recommends special revolvers (the Colt .38 is "very concealable," the Skolovsky .45 is "extremely accurate and durable"), silencers, and bulletproof vests.

The ultimate spy transport? "It just has to be James Bond's Aston Martin from the film *Goldfinger*. Who could forget 007's duel with the Ford Mustang as Bond pursued Goldfinger to his hideaway in Switzerland? That was some vehicle."

Finally, this whole encompassing "catalogue" analyses cryptography, codes, and ciphers and relates biographical data of well-known spies like the Russian Rudolph Abel who, masquerading as an artist, expanded the KGB spy network in the metropolitan New York area; the beautiful dancer Mata Hari, who used her charms to gain information and transmit it to German officers during World War I; and Gary Powers, an Air Force jet fighter pilot who was recruited by the CIA to fly the famous U-2 spy plane on reconnaissance missions over the Soviet Union.

The *Catalogue* ends with a glossary ("Spy Talk—A to Z") in which we learn the vocabulary of espionage, including the meaning of "Alimony" (compensation received by agents after they come out from being undercover in an unfriendly country), "Bag Job" (a secret entry, euphemism for breaking and entering, most often with the purpose of stealing or photographing material), "Big Daddy" (the National Security Agency), "Cobbler" (individual who creates forged passports), "Dog-and-Pony Show" (a meeting for top intelligence officials in order to provide pertinent information), "Shoe" (a fake passport), and "Spook" (spy).

Illustrated with over fifty photographs, *The Whole Spy Catalogue* is a compact yet thorough guide to espionage lore. (Amnon Kabatchnik)

Dick Francis. *Break In*. Fawcett, 1986.

It starts off with the gossipy little newspaper device which Francis has used in several other books, and the device has never been especially credible. To meet with it in yet another book, featured prominently from the first, is to meet with it once too often.

The following paragraph appeared in the *Daily Flag*, on the page entitled "Intimate Details," a page well known to contain information varying from stale to scurrilous and to be intentionally geared to stirring up trouble:

> Folks say the skids are under Robertson (Bobby) Allardeck (32), racehorse trainer son of tycoon Maynard Allardeck (50). Never Daddy's favorite (they're not talking), Bobby's bought more than he can pay for, naughty boy, and guess who won't be coming to the rescue. Watch this space for more.

Someone had pushed the paper through the letter boxes of "half the tradesmen in Newmarket," the paragraph outlined in red.

The phone rang off the hook at the Bobby and Holly Allardeck residence. Everyone they owed telephoned demanding to be paid. People made horrible threats about taking them to court. The feed merchant said the thirty horses in their stables could go without feed unless they paid him. The blacksmith said the horses would have to go without shoes unless they paid him. The owners of the thirty horses called non-stop, making veiled threats about taking their horses some place where there was feed and shoes. Luckily, Holly won some money on a race won by her twin brother, jockey Kit Fielding, and is able to pay the plumber.

All these things occurred on the first day. I find myself hard pressed to believe that the *Daily Flag* could stir up so much trouble for Bobby and Holly in twenty-four hours with the one paragraph above, which was libelous. Maybe I've underestimated the power of the press. And how did Bobby and Holly get everything on credit in this modern pay-me-instantly world?

The only thing that saved them was Kit's racing to the rescue.

The remainder of the book reached about the same level. The high points were the horse racing scenes.

My recommendation is never to miss a book by Dick Francis. (Frank Floyd)

Gerald Seymour. *Archangel.* Charter Books, 1983, 311 pp.

There is plenty about this book to turn the reader off, but don't let that happen to you. The beginning situation is a Cold War swap that doesn't come off--because the Russian agent in British hands dies suddenly. His British counterpart is whisked off to the Gulag. Except for scattered interesting bits about the British agent-hero's background, the rest of the first half bogs down in depressing detail of the plight of Russian prisoners that might have (may have?) come straight out of *A Day in the Life of Ivan Denisovitch.*

Then it gets interesting. Very.

The hero strikes back at evil authority. He sabotages the
camp commander's office. He poisons the water supply of the
guards' barracks. Finally, he leads the first open insurrection
of Russian prisoners.
     Naturally this is doomed to fail. But before it does,
through ingenuity and idealism, the rebels wreck tanks and
helicopters and hold their compound for longer than seems
possible against regular Russian troops.
     The last half of the book is as inspiring as the original
Rocky movie. In case you have forgotten in the flood of
sequels, that first movie was a paean to the indomitability of
the human spirit. (Jeff Banks)

Pierre Rey. *Out.* Bantam, 1980.

     This first U.S. edition of a French suspense thriller is an
interesting Mafia book. Appearing too late to ride the coat
tails of the major fad of Don Pendleton imitators (exhausted by
the late-mid 1970s), the rather concurrent publicity blitz for
either Godfather movie or any other discernable promotional
advantage, it must be that the Bantam editors felt it was strong
enough to stand alone. This reviewer's evaluation is a *maybe*.
     The Mafia people depicted are closer to the eccentrics of
Richard Condon's characters than to the usual stereotypes of
either the favorable or unfavorable sort. Yet while a *Prizzi's
Honor* (or sequel) succeeds in making us chuckle, the Mafiosos
of *Out* merely seem (to me) eccentric. The American cops
aren't quite the expected thing either, neither being heroic
successes nor comic failures. And while their ringing not-quite-
true may be mostly an index of how solidly the stereotypes have
been established, the most interesting thing about them to me--
and what I often find myself involuntarily focusing on in a
European book with American characters--is their *little* incon-
sistencies. Obviously this is not an important enough feature to
justify recommending the book.
     However, the non-Mafia European characters are a delight.
The wealthy young girl alternating her teasing talents between
her socialist fiance and her super-rich dad (and driving both
repeatedly to distraction), the greedy Swiss banker who dares to
steal *from* the Mafia, and several minor figures are real
treasures. Also, the two amoral women--one a prostitute and
the other "the next best thing"; one an African, the other an
American--are also tremendously funny.
     On top of that, the mystery element, launched with a
shock in the first scene that is too good to spoil by repeating
it here, is skillfully milked for a good half of the book. After
that the main suspense relates to who will finally wind up with
the $4 billion in "floating" Mafia money ... and *how*. Most
readers will probably be able to figure that out, too, but Rey's
telling it is skillful enough to make it worth reading to the end.
     Search this one out in the used-book stores! (Jeff Banks)

Lawrence Sanders.   *The Tenth Commandment.*   Berkley, 1983, $3.95.

Confession may be good for the soul. I know that when I went to Baylor (so long ago they couldn't afford decent football players) that mine were especially prized because I was not one of the True Believers. This one won't be spicy, however; just an admission that I have dipped into--well, allow me the odd *double entendre* figure of speech at least!--the works of most of those "big best-seller writers" whose formulas rely heavily on the staples of Mystery. Of them all, the one I keep coming back to with eagerness is Lawrence Sanders. Now, ordinarily I don't review his stuff (or in any other way trumpet "my secret sin"), but on occasion I can't resist. *The Tenth Commandment* is just such an occasion.

Its one-time hero, as opposed to the recurring retired police detective of the *Deadly Sin* books, is a law firm's investigator; this allies him closely to my favorite hero type (the private eye). The book's story is of two separate investigations which eventually are melded into one--a familiar private eye plot device. I should also mention that Erle Stanley Gardner, best known of course for his lawyer detective, did private detectives in his second most popular book series and at least one quite good pulp series about an investigator, Ed Burke, for a law firm (Small, Weston & Burke, introduced the same year he created Perry Mason).

Another plus is that both mysteries are quite good puzzles--in one a supposed suicide turns out to have been *almost* a locked room murder, and in the other a missing man is found dead--in both cases due to the perseverance of our hero. He also finds a hidden missing will, and (more typical of the "big best seller" school than of the private eye) works out his own love life satisfactorily after some rather predictable false starts.

One thing that does not work is the humor--mostly confined to giving major characters malapropian names. The diminutive hero is Mr. Bigg, the names of the senior partners in his firm contribute to an acronym (TORT), their office manager is Hamish Hooter, the hero's predecessor and mentor as investigator was named Roscoe, etc. Due to his (lack of) stature the hero is frequently subjected to midget jokes. The office beauty, Miss Apatoff, is a transparent gold digger. Yet the book is worthwhile and recommended. If, like me, you like Sanders, you will enjoy this book if you haven't already read it. And if you have, why didn't *you* review it and alert me to it sooner? (Jeff Banks)

Edward Acheson.   *The Grammarian's Funeral.*   Macrae Smith, 1935, 320 pp.

Choosing a book by its title is much like buying a pig in a poke. The contents are always a surprise--sometimes pleasant, sometimes disappointing, sometimes uncertain.

The Grammarian's Funeral turned out to be nothing like I imagined it would be. It is the story of Crane Adams, meek, mild, downtrodden, and abused by the principal of his school, his wife, his students, and almost anyone else he comes into contact with.

Adams's cousin, Chatterton Manley, to whom Adams owes a significant sum which he is paying back, apparently sporadically, disappears. Everybody but Adams is aware that Manley's wife is in love with him. Manley's suitcase is found in Adams's garage. All that the police are lacking is a corpse.

The arrest of Adams by the police as "a material witness," though they are sure he has done away with Manley, changes him from, if I may put it this way, a Casper Milquetoast to something like Mr. Hyde, although not quite as bright as the latter. Because of Adams's efforts--if blundering about does not describe it better--the corpse is found and the real murderer is unmasked.

Adams's alteration was unconvincing, as was the story that mumps in an adult male can cause impotence. But I was anticipating--why, I cannot say--a lighter, more frivolous novel from the title, and thus my judgment is probably suspect. (William F. Deeck)

Stewart Sterling. *Where There's Smoke.* Lippincott, 1946; Dell
    Mapback #275, n.d., 238 pp.

Saying that the Dell mapback has a great cover and leaving it at that is a temptation. But our noble editor has a strange notion that his readers should get their money's worth, so ever onward and downward.

A two-alarm fire at the Brockhurst Theater leads to the discovery of a body burned to death, although the chap would also have died shortly from drinking denatured alcohol. The fire was deliberately set. Whoever was after the poor guy, and apparently he had nothing but enemies, wasn't taking any chances.

Fire Marshal Ben Pedley investigates this fire and a later fire and is involved in a third one. He also--

--Is "barrelling" up "sleet greased" Broadway in New York at a "screaming" seventy miles per hour worrying about the equipment responding to the second alarm because "no driver could get up to speed" on those streets. He then bears down on the gas.

--Nearly dies in the first fire rescuing a damsel in distress.

--Is conked over the head and tied up while searching the dead man's apartment. (A killer, who later tries to do away with Pedley, does the conking and tieing. Why he doesn't get it over with then is only conjecture, but it's probably because there was still four fifths of the novel yet to come.)

--Nearly dies when the floor collapses under him while he is investigating a fire in progress.

--Lets a prisoner drive his car, rather than cuff the guy. ("Better this way," Pedley says smugly and erroneously. The

prisoner wrecks the car at fifty miles per hour. He escapes
unscathed, while Pedley gets a bruised thigh.)
     --Is shot at in a lawyer's office by the guy who didn't kill
him at the apartment. I'm taking the author's word for it here.
I'm still trying to figure out how and why it happened the way
he says it happened.
     --Is nearly drowned in the pool at a Turkish bath by the
guy who didn't try to kill him at the apartment and failed to
kill him at the lawyer's office.
     --Is laid out by a blow from a revolver butt to the bridge
of his nose.
     --Rescues again, more or less, the same damsel in distress
from another fire and comes close to being burned alive.
     One doesn't expect a novel to be completely realistic, but
there ought to be some connection with the real world.
     Fire-fighting buffs should stick to Dennis Smith. (William
F. Deeck)

John Lutz. *Tropical Heat.* Henry Holt, 1986, 246 pp., $14.95.

     The setting is central Florida and the private detective is
Fred Carver, a fortyish balding ex-cop whose police career
abruptly ended when he was kneecapped by a Latino street
punk.   A new protagonist and a new scene, but the world
caught on the pages of *Tropical Heat* is unmistakably the world
of John Lutz, the St. Louis area's foremost suspense novelist,
and the superficially tough and cynical Carver clearly belongs in
the post-Ross Macdonald fraternity (or is the word siblinghood?)
of concerned and compassionate PIs, right alongside Lutz's
earlier detective character, the timid and soft-hearted Alo
Nudger.
     Vegetating in the beachfront bungalow he bought with his
disability pay, Carver is visited by upscale real-estate sales-
person Edwina Talbot and in effect challenged to stop pitying
himself and do something with the rest of his life.   The
particular something she wants him to do is to find her lover,
Willis Davis, who in the middle of a solitary continental
breakfast on her terrace either walked out on her for no
reason, or jumped off a cliff into the ocean, or was pushed off.
The search leads Carver to a condominium time-sharing scam, a
drug deal (in Florida, what else?), an assortment of close calls,
and an emotional entanglement with his lovely and much-abused
client which neither he nor she is well equipped to handle.
     The plot of *Tropical Heat* is the bare-bones variety, but
the meat on those bones is prime Florida *noir.* Lutz does a
blazingly vivid job not only with the sun-soaked atmosphere and
the wild action scenes (including Carver's underwater duel with
a Marielito knife killer and an airboat chase through the
midnight Everglades) but also with the anguished relationship of
a man and a woman each struggling against a personal darkness.
This novel makes great summer reading--provided the reading is
done in an air-conditioned room to counteract Lutz's descriptions of the oppressive Florida heat. (Francis M. Nevins, Jr.)

James Ellroy.   *Suicide Hill.* Mysterious Press, 1986, 280 pp.,
$15.95.

Readers and moviegoers of the nineteen forties and fifties
didn't know it at the time, but they were living through the
first wave of the harsh, moody, downbeat suspense novels and
films we now describe as *noir.* Since around 1970 we've been
battered by a second wave of *noir* in print and on the screen--
Joseph Wambaugh, George V. Higgins, Elmore Leonard, James
Crumley, *Dirty Harry, The French Connection, Death Wish,
Chinatown, Taxi Driver, Body Double*--only this time the imagery
is in color, not black-and-white, the sex and violence are
graphic, not poetic, and the sense of sleaze is overpowering.
For better or worse, it's the books and films of the neo-*noir*
configuration that most vividly shape our perception of American
urban life today.

James Ellroy is part of that configuration. He was born in
1948 and marked forever at age ten when his mother was
strangled to death by a man she'd picked up in a bar.   He
drifted into the hippie-druggie subculture of the Vietnam years.
"From '65 to '77," he says, "I lived mostly on the streets,
flopping out in parks, with about fifty arrests for drunk,
trespassing, shoplifting, disturbing the peace, and other Mickey
Mouse, booze-related misdemeanors. I imagine I did a total of
about six months' county jail time.... I almost croaked from a
series of booze- and dope-related maladies early in '77.
Realizing that it was live or die, I opted for life.   I've been
sober since August of '77."   He began writing a year or two
later. *Suicide Hill* is his fifth novel in as many years and the
third of his police procedurals featuring L.A.P.D. detective
sergeant Lloyd Hopkins, Los Angeles' version of Dirty Harry.

The Hopkins books are contrapuntally structured, with the
alternation of perpetrator-cop-perpetrator-cop chapters borrowed
from Wambaugh's 1974 classic, *The Onion Field*, and are
punctuated with blood orgies borrowed from neo-*noir* movie
directors like Brian De Palma. By Ellroy's standards the first
half of *Suicide Hill* is quiet and almost sedate, introducing the
sleazeball cast--a white psycho, a Chicano psycho, the Chicano's
weak-willed kid brother, the coked-out porn video star by whom
the white psycho is obsessed, a call girl with a master's in
economics and a habit of reading George Gilder's capitalist
manifestos between tricks--and setting us up for confrontations
between each of these characters and Crazy Lloyd Hopkins. The
blood and brains flow in earnest during the book's second half,
with five gruesome killings between pages 149 and 168 alone, as
Hopkins comes closer and closer to the showdown which, for
weird reasons of his own, Ellroy never lets happen.

Crazy Lloyd is a walking time-bomb, clearly just as sick as
the pervs and perps he deals with. He routinely commits
burglary to obtain evidence and perjury to get convictions. He
fantasizes maiming the people he hates, such as a left-wing
lawyer or his estranged wife's new lover, and every so often he
makes good on his dreams. Ellroy draws all sorts of parallelisms
between cops and creeps, but at the same time he wants us to

accept Hopkins as a Jesus of the gutters, the way Wambaugh portrays his own police heroes. It's one of *Suicide Hill's* many weaknesses that Ellroy never fuses the two sides of his protagonist's character into a unity.

There are other problems, too: key scenes that are nearly incomprehensible, slipshod construction in spots, constant grammatical flubs that betray the white heat in which the book was written. And yet with all its faults this book has power. Ellroy is a master of the single most crucial neo-*noir* skill: he can make the nightworld of sleaze and street monsters come alive on the page. At one point he has a character "wondering if the world was nothing but wimps, pimps, psychos and sex fiends." For Ellroy, child of violence and the city, the answer is Yes, and so far he has not conjured up an effective redeemer. If you can stand the relentless assault, on every level from physical butchery to sex abuse to four-, ten-, and twelve-letter words to racist humor, this is a perversely fascinating evocation of a world gone mad. (Francis M. Nevins, Jr.)

Richard Rosen. *Fadeaway.* Harper & Row, 1986, 264 pp., $15.95.

Robert B. Parker may not be the best private eye writer of the eighties but surely he's the most influential, as witness the horde of newcomers to the field who have use his pretentious, wildly overrated, consistently best-selling series about the Boston PI Spenser as their takeoff point. Richard Rosen, winner of the Mystery Writers of America Edgar award for the best first crime novel of 1985, deserves another prize for using Parker most creatively.

The main character both in *Fadeaway* and in Rosen's prize-winning *Strike Three You're Dead* is a sort of Jewish Spenser, at least in the sense that each man is a smart-mouthed jock from Boston with a liberated live-in lady and a snootful of angst. Harvey Blissberg has turned hesitantly to the PI game after the early end of his career as a major-league outfielder, but he's not very good at his new line of work and all his cases seem to come to him from his sports world connections. In *Fadeaway* he's hired simultaneously by the Boston Celtics and the Washington Bullets to find out why a basketball star from each team vanished from Logan Airport within forty-eight hours of one another. When both players are found shot to death, Harvey follows the trail into the seamy world of college sports recruiting, and his hunch that the murders are tied in with the seven-year-old "accidental" death of a high school basketball champ in a dark bus tunnel stirs up the usual hornet's nest of corruption.

If Ross Macdonald had written this book, the plot would have been so convoluted you'd need a chart to sort out who did what to whom. Rosen goes to the opposite extreme, leaving out complexity and surprise almost entirely. If Parker had written the book, there would have been a violent confrontation in every chapter. Rosen avoids action scenes almost entirely, too. But he's an excellent stylist, with the ability to describe an

American city (in this case Providence, Rhode Island) and the
inner world of desperately lonely people as well as any PI
novelist now at work. What sets Rosen apart from everyone
else in the field, however, is his gift for shifting without effort
from the *film noir* gear into another mode entirely. Here for
example is Harvey anguishing over the case with his girlfriend,
Mickey:

> "I can't figure out where their lives crossed.
> Christ, Mick, what am I going to do? I'm out of my
> element."
> "You never had an element."
> "Thanks. You're joking and I'm having a crisis."
> "Life is a series of crises."
> "It hasn't always felt like this."
> "Okay, I take it back. Life is a series of crises
> separated by brief periods of self-delusion."
> "I need a pith helmet to protect me from your
> sayings."

Jock though he's supposed to be, Harvey is the only PI in the
literature who cries out to be played by Woody Allen.
  Fadeaway is crammed with scenes which are not only
hilarious in their own right but marvelous as parodies of the
tiresome philosophic shticks in the Spenser novels. It's light on
action and complexity, but the first-rate dialogue and charac-
terizations and the rich anti-Parker subtext make this one a joy
to read. (Francis M. Nevins, Jr.)

Thomas Hauser.   *The Beethoven Conspiracy.*   Macmillan, 1984,
    $13.95.

  Did classical giant Ludwig van Beethoven actually compose
a tenth symphony? Historical fact says no. Mystery writer
Thomas Hauser says yes, and uses it as the basis for the best
musical murder mystery since *The Mozart Score.*
  Hauser's protagonists are Judith Darr, a freelance violist,
and Richard Marritt, detective lieutenant of the N.Y.P.D. The
trail of murderous musicology leads them to a chateau high in
the Austrian Alps and a meeting of the archetypical demented
genius whose bitterness against the musical world is monumental.
The book proves to be informative on stringed instruments,
police procedure, and orchestral protocol, as well as being a
darned good mystery. It is a combination of "arts people" and
non-arts, and how the two learn to appreciate each other.
  The Beethoven Conspiracy is amusing, enjoyable, and
informative in a minor way. A good book perhaps for the pre-
concert wait on the lawn at Tanglewood. (Alan S. Mosier)

The Documents in the Case

(Letters)

From John M. Reilly, 25 West St. Albany, NY 12206:

I hasten to correct what you shrewdly inferred was an oversight. My check is enclosed for a renewal of subscription to born-again TMF. It is wonderful to have you back, released from the clutches of yet another professional school. Since the new practice of law education is to award the JD, do we now address you as Doctor Doctor?

The format of 9:1 aka 8:1 (inside cover [oops!]) is a genuine pleasure to read, but what's more it is very nice in the hand. We have known forever that printing was the technology that produced the first commodities for the bourgeois culture (mass produced books one can shove on a shelf without feeling bad about not giving them daily use or saving them up the heirs), so it has never seemed reasonable for folks to prefer production that looks like the machine is failing. Above all a mag devoted to the premier popular genre should look like a nice commodity. Fine job.

Let me also take the opportunity allowed by a few more inches of clean paper to say that I thoroughly enjoyed To Prove a Villain. Read it in one sitting and thumbed back through it in another. And yes, with Frank Floyd I found the prose attractive—written by an author who has pondered craft. Congratulations. [Thanks very much indeed for the kind words, but whatever value TPAV may have as prose, it apparently is lacking in persuasive power. Witness Marvin's apostasy in his column in this issue. Richarditis is the disease which will not die. No matter how many times a pro-Richard fallacy is debunked, the Richardists keep dragging it back to its feet again and pretending that it is brand new. There is nothing in Marvin's recitation of reasons for giving Richard the benefit of the doubt which is not addressed in TPAV, but a reading of Williamson's Mystery of the Princes evidently purged from his mind everything that he had learned from TPAV. I give up. To paraphrase an old saw, you can lead a Richardist to water, but you can't make him think.]

From William F. Deeck, 6020 Autoville Drive, College Park, MD
20740:

My thanks to Charles Shibuk for pointing out that Marv
Lachman had pioneered the "gems" type selections. And I had
thought that Marv was a mere slip of a lad. But he has been
around so long and done so much so well, I guess the safest
thing to do when attributing things to other people is always
add "and, of course, Marvin Lachman."
Speaking of Marv, his "It's About Crime" is, as usual,
outstanding. I would have said the same things about R. Austin
Freeman's *The Red Thumb Mark* that he did, but I would have
said them at much greater length, as is my custom, and would
not have captured the book as well as he did. Yes, some of the
prose is flowery, and the romance, if such it can be called, is a
bit sappy. But when one thinks of today's romances--an
exchange of blood tests and "wham-bam-thank-you-ma'am"--it's a
nice change of pace.
Which leads into Marv's review of Richard Stevenson's
Death Trick, or the "wham-bam-thank-you-Sam" school. Marv
says "it seems strange" that Stevenson would paint such an
unflattering picture of homosexual life. Unfortunately, that is a
flattering portrait. When there ain't much to brag about, you
brag about lots of sex with multiple partners. And in the light
of the 1981 date for the book's publication and our preoccupa-
tion with AIDS, one wonders whether Stevenson might now be
cringing a little.
In the discussion of reprints of older books, International
Polygonics and Academy Chicago should not be overlooked, nor
should Hogarth Press in England and now Penguin with its
Classic Crime reprint. All produce excellent editions. I bought
my copy of Freeman's *The Red Thumb Mark* in the Carroll &
Graf edition, but I'd rather have the Dover one, if truth be
known. And why can't those who reprint the older books get
together to avoid needless duplication in reprinting as was the
case with Freeman's book?
Is there a genre in which so much old stuff is brought
back in print? Does this say something about the quality of
today's mysteries? Does it say something about the quality of
old mysteries that apparently the past bestsellers in general
fiction didn't possess? I sure would like to see some thoughtful
people--Marv, are you listening?--comment on this trend.
Mike Nevins is fascinating as always on Cornell Woolrich.
So why do I feel so bloody depressed after reading an episode?
It was sad information about John Nieminski and Earl
Bargainnier. I met John for the first, and sadly the last, time
at the Baltimore Bouchercon. We discussed various things on
several occasions there. He pointed out, correctly, several
shortcomings of the convention organization, but he did it in
such a manner that there was nothing critical and I was left
pretty much with the feeling I had figured it all out by myself,
though far too late to do any good. I would certainly have
liked to know him better and was looking forward to Minneapolis to further that end.

As a comment on Ola Strom's "Abandoned Queens and Some Notes on Unintentional Plagiarism," allow me to quote, not plagiarize, from Bill Pronzini's marvelous *Gun in Cheek*, recently reissued by Mysterious Press in trade paperback, a study that should be owned by anyone claiming an interest in the mystery field or a sense of humor, and definitely by anyone who has both:

> Just one of the many remarkable things about *The Invisible Host* [by Gwen Bristow and Bruce Manning] is the fact that its plot is quite similar to Agatha Christie's *Ten Little Niggers* (also published at *Ten Little Indians* and *And Then There Were None*). This is made even more remarkable by the added fact that the Bristow/Manning opus was published nine years *before* the Christie. Dame Agatha is certainly above reproach and doubtless was unaware of the existence of, much less had read, *The Invisible Host* when she conceived her masterpiece; writers of her stature do not look elsewhere for inspiration. The truly fascinating point is that a team of young American writers and the British grand dame should have come up with essentially the same plot nine years apart and have made of it a pair of classic novels, one at each end of the mystery spectrum.

Good luck on the Nero Wolfe compendium, concordance, whatever. You can have the Nero Wolfe's World title if you want, particularly since I would have stolen it from Jaggard. You've got a customer in me when it's done.

From Mike Nevins, 7045 Cornell, University City, MO 63130:

It never fails. I knew that if I wrote asking you what happened to the latest TMF, my copy would come before my letter could reach you. Sure enough, the magic worked again!

And a fine issue too. Perhaps I can add a few tidbits to Ola Strom's article about the unwritten Ellery Queen novels. First of all, about what Fred Dannay called *The Indian Club Mystery*. I don't think it's coincidence that Indian clubs figure prominently in the denouement of Queen's 1938 novel *The Devil to Pay*, and I suspect that whatever Indian club gimmick he and Manny Lee dreamed up in their nationality-title period, 1929–1935, wound up in that second-period novel. Secondly, about the book Fred was working on when Manny died. One evening about ten years ago, when I was visiting Fred in Larchmont, he started talking about that book with me. I didn't have a tape recorder with me and was too caught up listening to take notes at the time, but I recall quite vividly the gist of what he said. He'd been reading the avant-garde psychotherapist R.D. Laing and was impressed with Laing's theory that the so-called insane are saner than the so-called normal people. The last of the unwritten EQs was to be built about the notion that all the

apparent crazies would turn out to be the truly sane ones and
the one apparently sane character would turn out to be nutty as
a fruitcake.   I knew of course that all the EQ novels after *The
Finishing Stroke* depended heavily on recycling motifs from
earlier EQs, and as Fred told me this storyline I remember
thinking that the next to be recycled was going to be *There
Was an Old Woman* (1943).   I can even recall that a line from
my description of that novel in *Royal Bloodline* ran through my
head: "Mad is sane, sane is mad, and we've all tumbled into the
rabbit-hole without knowing it."   Fred of course never did
anything with this plot after Manny's death, and we'll never
know whether it's just as well that he didn't.

There are a number of other cases of "simultaneous
inspiration" in the genre.   The exchange-of-murders idea which
most fans think of as having started with Patricia Highsmith's
Strangers on a Train goes back at least to 1938 and Asa Baker's
Mum's the Word for Murder.   Baker was an early pseudonym of
Davis Dresser, better known as Brst Halliday, the creator of
Mike Shayne.   The narrator-as-murderer gimmick we associate
with *The Murder of Roger Ackroyd* was used in 1923 in Leo
Perutz' *The Master of the Day of Judgment.*   The body-in-the-
rug notion from the Highsmith quotation stems from one of
Cornell Woolrich's first great noir short stories, "The Corpse
and the Kid," also known as "Boy with Body" (1935).   This kind
of thing has probably happened dozens of times in mystery
fiction alone and thousands of times in other areas of fiction.
Fred Dannay had a bit of a hang-up about priority of plot idea,
more so than any other writer I've met.   If he thought someone
else had come up with an idea first, he'd drop it like a hot
potato, and when he thought someone else had utilized an idea
from a Queen novel, he'd be more upset than most writers in
the same situation.   Of course, many others *did* borrow from
Queen, and sometimes a lot more than ideas.   Anyone remember
an NBC TV series called *Banacek* that ran from 1972-74?   One
of the last episodes of that series had to do with a crippled
airliner that vanished shortly after making an emergency landing
at a tiny desert airfield.   I watched that episode the night it
was broadcast, and so did Fred in Larchmont.   A few days later
he called me, wanted to know if I'd seen it and if I'd noticed
that the entire storyline bore a strong general similarity to the
storyline of one of the most famous Queen novelets, "The Lamp
of God" (1935).   I had.   We discussed whether he should sue for
copyright infringement, and after a while he agreed with me
that the *Banacek* episode was just different enough so that the
outcome of litigation would be a crap shoot.   Fred didn't believe
in spending money on gambles.   There was no suit, and the
episode can still be seen on late night reruns every now and
then.

From Jeff Banks, P.O. Box 13007 SFA Sta., Nacogdoches, TX
    75962:

Are you ready for my latest brainstorm?   Well, here it

comes anyway.

One of the things I always liked about TMF in the old days was its *clean look*. Lots of white space was what did it, and I know that this desirable appearance was paid for by "wasting" that space. And I know also that sometimes when an article ended only 6-15 lines down a page there was 3/4 (OR MORE) of a page of such wasted space.

Recently you have been "jumping" features to "continuation pages" and saving a great deal of space (and giving us readers more for our money!), but the looks of the publication have suffered.

What you need is fillers.

Remember the TAD of Hubin's editorship (back when TMF was starting up)? Of course you do. One of the Hubin features that his successors discontinued was a series of "Movie Notes." Almost without exception these served as fillers. They are something I miss a lot. Perhaps you could contact Bill Everson and get him to supply you with "Movie Notes" for TMF?

Failing that, here is my latest idea: I can probably supply you with 2-4 one-page (typescript) short pieces that I am calling "Mystery Mosts"; sometimes these would run less than a page, but I am proposing to put a one-page maximum limit on them—except for the first one, which would be used to "set the tone" and "establish" the series. After that, I would not even submit anything that spilled over onto a second page.

My typescript runs 220-260 words per page. Your printed pages in TMF (using a sampling of 8 pages on which I counted words from the last two issues) run 540-649 words. Therefore, my "filler-feature" would typically "fill" approximately 1/2 page spots.

I enclose three "Mystery Mosts" to give you an idea, and (incidentally) as my first submissions in the series. Actually, two of these suggest obvious follow-ups, and I would not want you to think there was any shortage of potential material. In fact, I have a notebook with a dozen—no, 13, I just counted—partially done "Mystery Mosts" and a list of 18 other things to research.

B O U C H E R C O N   X V I I I

MURDER IN THE NORTH COUNTRY

Ritz Hotel
Minneapolis, Minnesota
OCTOBER 9,10,11 1987,

GUEST OF HONOR

LAWRENCE
BLOCK

Matt Scudder

Bernie Rhodenbarr

-- Toastmasters --

Max Allan Collins & M.S. Craig

OTHERS EXPECTED TO ATTEND INCLUDE: *Bill Pronzini, Marcia Muller, Sara Paretsky, Herb Resnicow, Otto Penzler, Bill Crider, Robert J. Randisi, Linda Barnes, Allen J. Hubin, Dominick Abel, Ed Gorman, Kate Green, Edward Hunsburger, Teri White, Michael Seidman, L. A. Taylor, Doug Hornig, Francis M. Nevins jr., Guy Townsend, Joe L. Hensley, Ruth Cavin, Warren Murphy, R. D. Zimmerman, Mary Logue, Stephen Cohen, Harold Adams, Molly Cochran, Bill DeAndrea, Barbara Michaels-Elizabeth Peters, John Lutz, Loren D. Estleman, Jonathan Gash, Ian Stuart-Malcolm Gray & **many more***

HIGHLIGHTS: -- a film program; a benefit auction (for the Give the Gift of Literacy Foundation), the Anthony Awards, the PWA Awards; *a full day of alternate **Sherlockian** programming* - *with* John Bennett Shaw *to celebrate the* **Sherlock Holmes** *centenary;* a Saturday night banquet (separate registration required), a panel of spouses - to tell *their* side; scheduled autograph sessions, the Western side of Crime Fiction; the Midwest Mystery Scene, and the Canadian Crime Scene ... (***plus more*** ...)

Registration : $25.00 until July 1st - $35.00 thereafter ...Supporting membership $10.00

WRITE: BOUCHERCON XVIII, P. O. BOX 2747, LOOP STATION, MINNEAPOLIS, MINNESOTA 55402